:

HOW TO INTERPRE

A concise guide to the basic tec
and chart synthesis that provide
interpretative skills e

Also in this series:

ASTROLOGER'S COMPANION
John & Peter Filbey

ASTROLOGICAL COUNSELLING
Christina Rose

ASTRONOMY FOR ASTROLOGERS
John & Peter Filbey

CHART SYNTHESIS
Roy Alexander

CHINESE ASTROLOGY
Derek Walters

DRACONIC ASTROLOGY
Pamela A. F. Crane

FORECASTING BY ASTROLOGY
Martin Freeman

HARMONIC CHARTS
David Hamblin

HORARY ASTROLOGY
Derek Appleby

HOW TO RECTIFY A BIRTH CHART
Laurie Efrein

JUNGIAN BIRTH CHARTS
Arthur Dione

MUNDANE ASTROLOGY
Michael Baigent, Nicholas Campion & Charles Harvey

NATAL CHARTING
John Filbey

SYNASTRY
Penny Thornton

TWELVE HOUSES
Howard Sasportas

HOW TO INTERPRET A BIRTH CHART

A Guide to the Analysis and Synthesis
of Astrological Charts

by

Martin Freeman, D.F.Astrol.S.

THE AQUARIAN PRESS

First published 1981

© MARTIN FREEMAN 1981

British Library Cataloguing in Publication Data

Freeman, Martin
How to interpret a birth chart
1. Horoscopes   2. Astrology
I. Title
133.5'4   BF1728

ISBN 0-85030-249-8

*The Aquarian Press is part of the Thorsons Publishing Group,
Wellingborough, Northamptonshire, NN8 2RQ, England.*

Printed in Great Britain by Woolnough Bookbinding Limited,
Irthlingborough, Northamptonshire.

5   7   9   11   13   15   14   12   10   8   6

CONTENTS

		Page
Introduction		7
Chapter		
1.	The Horoscope	11
2.	Approaches to Interpretation	14
3.	The Planets	18
4.	The Signs	32
5.	More About the Signs	51
6.	The Houses	59
7.	Planets in the Signs and Houses	68
8.	The Aspects	94
9.	Miscellanea	115
10.	Final Words	120
	Table of Keywords	122
	Index	125

INTRODUCTION

In my experience of teaching astrology students at all levels, the question which is raised time and time again concerns the art of synthesis. Analysing a horoscope is comparatively easy. The beginner first probably uses a range of text books to gain a consensus interpretation of each placing in the chart and then, as he or she gradually learns the principles, each separate interpretation can be given from personal knowledge. But the next step, from analysis to synthesis, often appears formidable, as though a wide chasm lies across the path. The student may feel frustrated and inadequate and wish for a pair of magical seven-league boots to help him over the barrier.

Analysis of the chart provides the pieces of the jigsaw; synthesis enables one to put them together so that they fit comfortably and show a coherent, interesting and helpful picture. I hope that this book will make it easier for the student to take that step towards the art of synthesis. Part of a series, this volume draws together some of my personal views about astrological interpretation, gathered after many years of studying the subject and of working as an astrological consultant. It also reflects some of what I have learned by teaching, and I hope this act of sharing will be a positive contribution to the furtherance of sound astrological knowledge.

It is not a large book and, as such, is limited in its scope; but it represents an up-to-date, handy-sized volume on natal chart interpretation which will be of value in any astrologer's library. Its aims are relatively simple. Anyone who has a properly drawn up birth chart, and who has assimilated what is contained in the book, should be able not only to achieve a basic interpretation of the chart, covering all the normally-used significators, but also to move towards a synthesis of the chart's meaning, a deeper insight into what lies behind the conventional textbook interpretations.

However, no single book (let alone one of this size) can provide all the answers to astrological interpretation, and the art of synthesis is a skill which cannot be acquired instantly through specific study or by learning certain formulae. It grows with experience and maturity—but there are certain attitudes of mind, pointers and pathways, which will lead more quickly in that direction. These are what this book hopes to indicate, by offering hints here, highlights there and, where possible, presenting standard astrological information in a synthesized, rather than compartmentalized manner.

My own interest is in astrology as a tool for self-understanding and psychological development. Potentially, the chart shows all the character material which is available to the individual. Not all of it is likely to be conscious and there are different ways in which that material can be used, but study and understanding of what the chart represents will always help any person to know himself or herself better. It can help to bring what is unconscious into consciousness and, as this process develops, the individual will start to unfold his own reality, learning to accept that he is who he is and discovering how to use his potential effectively. The most important chart reading which any astrologer does will always be his or her own—and it will also be the longest, lasting for a lifetime.

I do not believe that astrology works because a complexity of cosmic rays imprint on a baby's head as it emerges into the world, creating a pattern of character and life-development. Perhaps when scientific enquiry moves properly into para-science, subtle forces will be discovered which may show that there is an answer of this nature, but at the moment we are not equipped to understand on such a level, if it exists. My own understanding of astrology falls in the area of holistic symbolism—C. G. Jung's principle of synchronicity is the most satisfactory way of explaining it. Whatever happens in a moment of time takes on the quality of that moment. If we can understand the symbolic meaning of the way in which the heavens were arrayed at a certain moment, then potentially we can understand the meaning of whatever happened at that moment—and one of the most complex of all the happenings is the start of a human being's life.

Many astrologers (including myself) believe in reincarnation. Although it may not be an acceptable belief for everyone, it deserves consideration, for the two subjects fit well with each other. If the soul is that constant undying unit within each individual, then each lifetime is merely one small part of a much greater process. The belief is that in past lives the soul has experienced many things, developed certain skills and no doubt made a few mistakes. It is older and wiser than one person can be in a single lifetime, and with that wisdom it is said to choose the next life to be led. If this is the case, then, in effect, each person chooses the social and economic environment to be born into, the sex, the parents, the inherited characteristics and the moment of birth, thus also choosing the chart as a map of the potential for that life. (This is valid for a natural birth, but argument occurs in the case of induced births. Either the chart is not quite as chosen—or the soul decided on a lifetime with the added complication of an induction).

Belief in reincarnation encourages much more tolerant attitudes to one's fellow men, for it is difficult to judge whether a person is making a good job out of a difficult life or making a mess out of an easy one. Also, fate and free will are put somewhat into proportion—the soul chooses the life (fate), but that life can unfold in many different ways (free will). For example, in a strongly Sagittarian chart, the individual may be fated to be very non-Cancerian, but he has free will in the way he expresses his Sagittarian qualities.

Any serious study of astrology which does more than scratch the surface will quickly plunge the student into deep philosophical and mysterious realms, but the subject always remains firmly based in the reality of the structure of the solar system. So astrology has the unique position of being a bridge between the technical and the symbolic, between factual reality and the non-rational and ultimately perhaps between science and religion. It is an age-old subject, which may have had its ups and downs in history, but it is one which resolutely refuses to go away.

Thus astrology is well grounded in the consciousness of the human race and is deeply rooted in the collective unconscious —and, to continue with Jungian terminology, it takes on the quality of an archetype. The study of astrology enables us to make contact with this ancient storehouse of energy and knowledge on many levels, some conscious, others unconscious. A person reading a sun sign column in a newspaper touches it unknowingly, but the serious student on a longer astrological journey can dig deeply into this source and will discover many treasures of inestimable worth.

1.
THE HOROSCOPE

It is important that the astrologer understands the reality of the horoscope or birth chart, for this is the factual point from which the interpretation starts, the foundation of the bridge which will span the gap between science and astronomy on one side and the sensitivities of human understanding on the other. The horoscope of an individual is merely a map of the heavens, drawn up for a moment in time—that moment at which the person took their first breath and physiologically started life independent from their mother. The map is drawn with the Earth at the centre and the Sun, Moon and planets seen in their various places in the sky relative to the Earth.

It helps to understand what the horoscope really is—and the place which our solar system takes in the vastness of space—if we first imagine being in a space ship far away on the edge of the universe. Stretching out into the infinite distance drift galaxies, swirls of clustered stars hanging in space like specks of dust in a sunbeam that shines into a deserted room. If we steer the space ship towards that galaxy which happens to be our own, we can focus attention on a certain star, not especially large and placed near the edge of the cluster. That star is our Sun, and as we approach it we see that it has satellites of its own, spinning around it in moving equilibrium, caught by its gravitational field. The satellites are the planets, and such is their pattern of movement that, viewed from the side, we would see the lines of their orbits like a disc, thin and flat. Viewed from above our solar system looks something like Figure 1—not to scale and with the irregularities removed. Thus, viewed from Earth, the Sun, Moon and planets appear to travel on the same broad path, as if along the rim of a giant wheel around the Earth. In very simple terms, the solar system is a flat, two-dimensional phenomenon and our horoscope or map reflects this.

Figure 1. Schematic diagram of the solar system (as it was at Prince Charles' birth).

The signs of the zodiac as used in the tropical zodiac are merely twelve divisions, each of 30°, along that apparent wheel-like path of the planets around Earth. They do not correlate exactly with the constellations of the same name, but are measured from the First Point of Aries—an astronomical point in space used by astronomers, navigators and astrologers alike. So our picture of the solar system in Figure 1 would appear in the horoscope as Figure 2 (the positions used are those for Prince Charles' birth).

The solar system is in constant motion. The Moon circles the Earth every 27⅓ days, while the Earth and the other planets circle the Sun in varying periods. Thus, in the horoscope, the Sun viewed from Earth appears to move around the complete zodiac in a year—about one month per sign. The Moon takes two or three days to pass through a sign, while the far distant planets, Uranus, Neptune and Pluto can take between 7 and 32 years per sign. So the horoscope is in constant motion as the planets, seen from Earth, travel through the signs at their different appointed speeds.

There is also a second movement in the horoscope caused by the

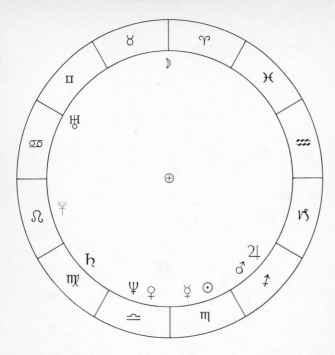

Figure 2. Simplified horoscope or map of the heavens (as at Prince Charles' birth).

rotation of the Earth. Imagine a day in early spring. The Sun is seen from the Earth to be in the sign of Aries. At dawn on that day—sunrise—the Sun, and that part of the zodiac wheel known as Aries, appear over the eastern horizon. At noon the Sun and Aries are somewhere high in the sky and another section of the zodiac, probably Cancer, is rising over the horizon. At sunset, Aries also sets over the western horizon and the opposite sign Libra will be rising in the east. At dawn the next day the Sun and Aries again appear to rise, but the Sun has moved a small distance (about a degree) through the sign. The other planets and the Moon will also have moved different distances through the zodiac.

The rising sign or Ascendant is an important feature of the horoscope, both in interpretation and as the point from which the twelve houses are counted. It is covered in more detail later in the book. But at this stage it is only important to know that there are always two movements going on within the horoscope—planets through the signs and apparent daily rotation around the earth.

2.
APPROACHES TO
INTERPRETATION

Once the basics of calculation* have been mastered, the serious student usually finds that interpreting the horoscope in depth is the most difficult feature of astrology. The birth chart presents a mass of information—wide ranging, paradoxical, complex and often conflicting. It is indeed a daunting task to both analyze and synthesize this data so that a character reading can be presented to a person in such a way that it is both helpful and understandable. But if the birth chart is to genuinely reflect that complexity which is a human being, then the information which it gives and its interpretation must be a complicated process. However, we can approach the subject methodically and simply and this will help us to find an easy path through the maze.

There are the following four basic ingredients in the chart:

The Planets
Basic principles of experience or life energies. Everyone has all of them in the chart, but they express in different ways and with varying strengths.

The Signs
Styles or modes of expression. These are the lenses through which the planetary energies filter and shine, taking on varying shades and intensities. All the signs are in each chart, but with different degrees of emphasis.

The Houses
Fields of activity or areas of experience. The houses cover the whole spectrum of life involvement, but each house assumes different levels of importance in different charts.

---

* These are dealt with in another book in this series, John Filbey's *Natal Charting* (Aquarian Press, 1981).

The Aspects

Linking forces between planets. The aspects create a dynamic structure within the chart.

Thus each unit of interpretation is simply a planetary energy expressing through a particular sign, focussing in the affairs of the house in which it is placed and linking to the rest of the chart by aspect.

There are ten planets (astrologers realize that the Sun and the Moon are not planets in the astronomical sense, but they are referred to as such for convenience) and there are twelve signs and houses where they may be placed. So the various combinations are enormous, even before the myriad aspect possibilities are considered. There are alternative ways of approaching the interpretation of this data and each individual will tend to develop an approach which suits him in particular ways and uses his skills appropriately and satisfactorily. But I advise each student to start off with a methodical system using keywords for the basic astrological ingredients. Some types of people can easily develop and refine the keyword system so that it becomes an efficient interpretation device, in tune with what will almost certainly be their practical, logical and organized approach to life. They will be at home with analysis, structure and categorization and will find it easy to build up the astrological chart interpretation brick by brick, starting with broad foundations upon which to place the main structure and completing the work with appropriate detail and enhancement. Chart interpretation by computer attempts to do this, but the bricks are placed methodically one on top of each other without any aesthetic appreciation—any attempts at linking, cross-referring and synthesizing have an unavoidable mechanized sterility. The methodical keyword approach to interpretation must have the human touch, but an astrologer using this approach will always be able to produce correct and straightforward interpretations.

Astrology is a subject which potentially not only reaches into all areas of experience, but also has the capacity to create a linking system within them. It deals essentially with human beings, offering insight into their true character, their paradoxes and their life possibilities. Sensitive and helpful astrological interpretation is fluid and integrative. There are many people who find it easier to look upon themselves as being made up of separate character compartments, but this is undesirable since it contributes to a lack of integration within their psyches and limits their potential. Rigid adherence to the keyword system aggravates this tendency, in client and astrologer alike.

To someone whose way of experiencing and evaluating life is based on feeling and intuition the keyword system can only be a temporary structure, a means to an end, which will no longer be required when the skills have been developed to enable a synthesized interpretation to flow smoothly and readily after study of the chart. Experience and practice will contribute greatly to this maturity of interpretation, coupled with the attitude to astrological knowledge that a serious astrologer never stops learning, soaking up information, using it within and applying it in the world.

Pure analysis of the birth chart is comparatively easy and anyone, perhaps even a computer, can make a reasonable job of it. Synthesis, pulling together all the multi-coloured threads into a unique weave, is a more elusive skill and is touched on at various points within this book. For the moment let the student concentrate study not just on astrology alone, important though that may be, but in two other areas as well. The first is 'people-watching', for human beings and their life experiences make up 90 per cent of astrology. Conscious observation and awareness of how people live their lives, why they behave in the ways they do and what their motivations are, all develop interpretative skills. The second is examination of oneself. The greater a person's self-awareness, the more in tune he will be with his own reality and purpose. This will better equip him to interpret with insight, to escape those blind spots which cause a person to miss in others what he cannot see in himself, and to avoid the trap of introducing personal value judgements to the interpretation of the chart of another separate, individual human being.

But however the interpretation is developed, the student must remember that the birth chart is a map of potential. The possibilities latent in the chart do not occur automatically, they have to be drawn out and used to the full, in the same way as a single hand of cards can be played with varying degrees of success. Because the chart's plain reality is only a map of the heavens for a moment in time, then its symbology can apply to any creation which occurred at that moment—a human being, a desk, a siamese cat, a business organization, or whatever. The siamese cat unquestionably has a greater opportunity to manifest the potential of the chart than the desk, but it has much less potential than the human being. The business organization will have an oblique or different potential and its 'consciousness' may be at varying levels. A pragmatist would no doubt contend that the desk has no potential and the business no consciousness; an esotericist would hold that everything lives, even apparently 'inanimate' objects. But the important point is that as far as human beings are concerned, they are all at different levels of consciousness and therefore have different opportunities for realising the potential of their charts. There is no way of knowing what that level is from the horoscope itself and so the interpretation must be presented with awareness of this fact and with skill and sensitivity.

3.
THE PLANETS

All the ingredients which go to make up astrological interpretation are symbols—not merely signs or labels. The latter merely provides a finite amount of information about a particular characteristic or quality, but are always subordinate to what they point to or describe. Symbols, on the other hand, possess an ever-expanding potential and are always greater than we can comprehend at the first meeting; therefore, they carry us forward to further understanding in the same way that a river carries a craft, now fast now slow, past ever-changing scenery, eventually to lead to the ocean—vast and unfathomable, but in some way knowable to the earnest searcher.

And yet study of each individual ingredient—planet, sign or house—still retains a feeling of categorization about it, leaning more towards analysis and compartments rather than the goal of synthesis which we seek. Thus, it is helpful to be continuously aware throughout our studies of the connections and groupings which exist in astrology in so many ways.

For example, there are various inter-relationships between the planets which we can consider. The Sun and the Moon have the greatest visibility and impact physically on the Earth and can be considered in some ways as a pair. The Sun brings warmth and light, always appearing as a golden disc in the sky. As a god he is powerful and masculine, constant in his energy giving. His moods and colour change only as a result of Earth's atmosphere—clouds, fog, evening haze—and when Earth turns half circle we feel the lack of his presence in darkness and chill. The Moon is the closest body to our planet, shiningly visible at night, cloud-textured by day and always changing in appearance through each month. She is a goddess—feminine, receptive, mysterious, influencing the earth's watery masses in the ebb and flow of the tides.

If we use the analogy of a family, Sun and Moon are like father and mother in our planetary order. Between the two of them in space lie the orbits of Mercury and Venus, son and daughter. Mercury, the young boy, eager to learn, posesses a quicksilver quality earning him the job of messenger of the Gods. Venus is Aphrodite, the beautiful daughter, desirous of love and relationship.

Beyond Earth's orbit is Mars, the red planet. He is the elder son who has gone out into the world to seek his fortune, carrying his sword in his hand. These five make up the immediate planetary family and they can be regarded as having the most personal influence on the birth chart. None takes more than two months to pass through a zodiac sign (the Moon takes only a few days) and all of them change their positions in the chart quickly, creating continuous differentiation as the weeks pass.

Beyond Mars lie the asteroids, rocky rubble which may once have been a solid planet, and beyond the asteroids are Jupiter and Saturn. These two bodies, largest planets in our solar system, are the most distant which can be seen by the naked eye. In the planetary family Jupiter is the jovial uncle, always optimistic and great fun to be with. He likes to bring gifts, even if he cannot afford to, and although the children love him, if he overstays his welcome his exuberance can be exhausting. Saturn is grandfather, a schoolmaster who never retired; strict and disapproving of the younger generation, he appears formidable to the young and immature. But he has much wisdom which he will share when approached with respect.

Saturn and Jupiter are like two great social balancing forces, conservation and expansion. They act as a link between the busy world of the planetary family, the personal planets, and the wider issues of the collective, the destiny of the human race, symbolized by the outer planets.

These planets, Uranus, Neptune and Pluto, were discovered after the invention of the telescope and probably John Keats was thinking of Uranus, first seen shortly before his birth, when he wrote (of Chapman's *Homer*): 'Then felt I like some watcher of the skies/When a new planet swims into his ken'. The exciting realization that Saturn was *not* the limit of the solar system must have fascinated many of the creative minds of that time. These outer planets are beyond any analogy of a planetary family, being more like a New Age Trinity for the human race, Magi offering gifts of enlightenment, inspiration and transformation.

Now let us consider each of the planets individually and in more detail.

The Sun

The Sun represents the basic urge for conscious self-expression in the chart. It is the solar energy cell in a person's character, the lord and giver of life, and symbolizes the way in which that individual will shine out to the world. The Sun is a person's sense of identity and the ease or assuredness with which he will be able to project his individuality will depend on the harmony of the aspects to the Sun and the extent to which the Sun's placing either balances or conflicts with other factors in the chart.

The Sun is a masculine principle and has to do with courage, power, self-confidence and will. It symbolizes authority and purpose, the ruler, father and husband; its potential is the peak of constructive maturity. Generosity, vitality and creativity spring from its source. The Sun is self-sufficiency in abundance, with energy enough to radiate warmth and life to all around.

The symbol for the Sun ☉ is like a diagram of a solar system, a cell or an atom, implying the power and creativity which the Sun represents in the chart. The single point in the centre is the seed, the first spark of life, the one dimensional essence from which all life grows. The circle is wholeness, the never ending flow of energy, which offers the goal of the individuated self as a possibility for everyone. The circle itself is often referred to as spirit. All creation can be seen in this one symbol, reminding us of the divine unity which promises that each one of us is God in potential.

Ancient man worshipped the Sun and ascribed numerous deities to the powerful golden orb in the sky. Such Gods as Ra, Apollo, Helios, Shakuru, Shamash and Osiris have names to conjure with. As the sounds roll off the tongue, we release the power of the archetypes. We can see Khepri, the Scarab God, pushing the ball of the Sun before him or we see visions of fiery chariots streaming across the sky as the Sun Gods make their inevitable daily journeys.

Sun Keywords: Identity, conscious self-expression, power, authority.

The Moon

The Moon in the sky shines with the reflected light of the Sun. In astrology it corresponds with the way in which we reflect and respond to what is going on around us. It has to do with our feelings, emotions and instincts and, in the same way in which the Moon influences the tides on our planet, so it symbolizes the ebb and flow of our emotional nature, our moods and changeability. It is the archetype of the mother, which is within us all, man or woman, if we care to find it; for it is through the Moon that we express parental instincts—caring, protectiveness and sensitivity. The Moon is said to have links with the past and it is from this almost primitive source that our natural instinctual responses flow. The Moon is a feminine principle and associates with the inner personality, receptiveness, passivity. It can act as inner guide to the deeper unconscious, a figure half-shrouded in mystery, linking the dark personal world of the unconscious to the clearer world of personal awareness.

The symbol for the Moon ☽ is a representation of its crescent in its waxing phase from new to full. But it can also be seen as two half circles. These form a bowl shape, a receptacle, a feminine container shaping anything which is put into it. The half circle itself, unlike the full circle, is finite and incomplete, almost as if striving for wholeness. It is often described as representing the soul—a statement which should not be taken literally, but which symbolically shows again the connecting quality of the Moon, here between the solar potential of spirit and the more extraverted, grounded elements of the chart.

In mythology the Moon is associated with both male and female deities, but it is Moon goddesses who symbolize more appropriately the astrological lunar principles and the archetype of the feminine —Isis, mother goddess; Artemis, associated with nature; Parvati, a Hindu goddess of fertility and feminine power; and Hecate, mystery, magic and darkness.

Moon Keywords: Response, receptivity, instinct, emotions, moods.

The Sun and Moon form the basic integration of masculine and feminine in the chart—yin-yang, active-passive. This is the inner relationship where a harmonious mariage within leads to psychological integration without. Similarly in outer relationship, in the comparison of horoscopes (synastry), we look for aspect links or sign sympathies between the Moon in one chart (the man's particularly) and the Sun in the other chart. In any relationship, knowing the Moon sign helps us understand the receptivity of the other person—'talk to their Moon sign' is always good advice. The mature adult, when in his postive phase, will use and exhibit his Sun sign characteristics. But where the ego is not yet formed, the small child will often show Moon sign qualities more strongly than other chart factors. This is because every action in the first two or three years of life is a reaction, a response to the bewilderingly exciting kaleidoscope of the immediate environment—new sights, new sounds, new smells and new tactile sensations. The little person has not yet developed the self-identity of the Sun.

Mercury

Mercury represents communication in all its forms—talking, reading, writing, teaching and thinking. The linking process provided by the carrying of messages is symbolized by Mercury and 'busyness' is the planet's hallmark. Indeed its very passage through the zodiac reflects its busy-body quality—Mercury is now ahead and now behind the Sun, around which it is orbiting as its closest satellite, but it is never more than 28° away. In the birth chart, Mercury indicates the mentality and intellectual capacity of the individual, how he talks, how he thinks and the ways in which his minds works. It points to reasoning abilities, to teaching and learning capacities and, in evolved manifestation, the transformation of spiritual energies into matter. The versatility and inquiring nature of Mercury take us back to the idea of the child in our planetary family—he is eager to learn and is interested in everything, but in the same way that a child before puberty has only a nominal interest in gender identity, so Mercury is considered to be neutral or hermaphrodite and its qualities tend to be especially coloured, not only by its sign and house placing, but also by any other planet making and aspect to it.

In appearance, the symbol for Mercury ☿ almost looks like a little mannikin with pricked up ears—alert and eager to pass on information. Symbolically it consists of the circle of spirit over the cross of matter, surmounted by the half circle of soul—a combination open to various interpretations, all of which may help to broaden our understanding of the planet's principles. Perhaps spirit is grounded in matter through the intuitive quality of the soul; perhaps the accumulation of memories of the many incarnations which a soul possesses is supreme over both spirit and matter where the mercurial quality of active intelligence is concerned. The symbol can also be seen as a representation of the caduceus, the magical baton with two snakes entwined around the shaft, sometimes topped with a winged symbol. The caduceus is a complex symbol worthy of further study, but in simple terms it represents the power of wisdom which can bring happiness and good fortune. It protects messengers, who traditionally carried it, and it also has important connections with healing, to-day being used as an emblem of the medical profession.

The god Mercury was Roman, but the counterpart in the Greek pantheon was Hermes. He was equipped with winged helmet and sandals and acted as messenger of the gods. He watched over all travellers and was the god of commerce, gambling and trickery. Teutonic Woden (Odin in Nordic mythology) although a war god, is associated with Mercury, as is Thoth in ancient Egypt.

Mercury Keywords: Communication—the written and spoken word, intellect, the mind.

Venus

Venus is the planet of relationship, harmony and beauty. Its placing in the chart shows the urge towards close personal attachment, the ability to love and the ability to be loved. It also indicates appreciation of art and beauty and it is one of the pointers towards creativity in the chart. Attraction is a powerful force and Venus uses it with feeling and energy. Although the planet is a feminine principle, it is not necessarily passive—consider the ardour of a young woman in love. Venus can express passionately, sensuously and extravagantly, but also with charm and beauty. Ancient astrologers referred to Venus as 'the lesser benefic'.

The symbol ♀ suggests that there is a balance between the cross of matter and the circle of spirit, but that spirit is supreme. More prosaically, one can see the symbol as the hand-held mirror in which the young woman admires herself. It is also the biological symbol for female.

Roman Venus was Aphrodite to the Greeks and watched over love, sensual pleasures, fertility and beauty. She was born out of the sea where Ouranos' severed genitals had fallen. Other love goddesses include Ishtar (Assyrio-Babylonian) and Frija, Freya or Frig (Celtic-Teutonic). The latter was fond enough of beautiful necklaces to spend a night with each of a number of dwarf craftsmen in order to obtain one which she particularly admired.

Venus Keywords: Love, attraction, beauty, harmony.

Mars

Mars is the symbol of energy, drive, assertiveness and aggression. Because it is such a powerful planet, the energy can often be polarized in its expression. The warrior can run wild on an undisciplined foray of pillage, rape and cruelty, whereas in a well-trained army the power is under control and can be directed with efficiency and discipline. The channelled energy of the planet brings out the courageous and assertive aspect of the masculine principle—confrontation is direct and confident, action is strong and effective. Mars commands respect when used harmoniously, but it only needs a slight loss of control for this energy to provoke fear, resentment and hatred. Initiative and independence come from Mars, actions which often imply a cutting loose from past patterns and restrictive comforts. Indeed Mars associates with all cutting edges, not only warriors' swords, but knives, scalpels and other sharp instruments.

The symbol for Mars once appropriately used to be the reverse of Venus and was drawn as the cross above the circle ♂. This was modified to the phallic, aggressive symbol in use today ♂, representing masculine in biology and iron in physics. The older symbol puts material considerations (the cross) above spirit (the circle)—spiritual matters can be entirely forgotten in the search for material achievement or, alternatively, it may show that the spiritual life still has to be lived in the material world, where the traveller needs courage and assertiveness for survival and progress.

Deities associated with the Mars principle are heroes and gods of war. Mars, the warrior god, was more important to the conquering Romans than equivalent Ares was to the Greeks. It was Mars who fathered Romulus and Remus, founders of Rome. Odin (Woden or Wotan) was the Nordic war god and Hercules, an archetypical hero, also symbolizes the Mars principle in the horoscope.

Mars Keywords: Energy, drive, confrontation, assertiveness.

Jupiter

Jupiter is the largest planet in the solar system and takes about a year to travel through one of the signs, and therefore about twelve years to make a complete cycle of the zodiac. It rotates fast on its axis spinning once every ten hours and is largely made up of gaseous substances—it also physically radiates energy, unlike most other planets which absorb energy. Appropriately, expansion, on a grandiose scale, is the principle of Jupiter in the horoscope. It is the planet of optimism, of manifold possibilities and of the wide horizons—new worlds to explore, new philosophies to enrich the mind and wider understanding of spiritual consciousness leading to wisdom. Jupiter used to be known as 'the greater benefic' and is often considered to bestow benevolence and good fortune on all its contacts. Certainly it tends to bring out the best of the sign and house in which it is placed, for enjoyment, preservation and happiness are its qualities. But sometimes Jupiter brings too much of a good thing—over enjoyment of food leads to expansion of the waistline, too much religious zeal brings not only long sermons, but fanaticism as well; excessive enthusiasm and opportunism can result in disappointment or even disaster. As with any astrological factor, channelling the energy is all important. Where Jupiter is not especially well placed in the chart, its energy can go cheerfully out of control. It is with patience and maturity that the primrose path becomes the wide road to wisdom.

The symbol itself is optimistic ♃ —the moon-like half circle of soul rises a little above the cross of matter and suggests a higher wisdom over material things.

In mythology, the Roman god Jupiter, Zeus to the Greeks and parallel deities in other cultures sometimes appear more powerful even than the Sun gods—perhaps because these beings are never depicted as remote. Wisdom, learning and justice were their attributes; thunder and lightning their visible power. Thor-Donar (Teutonic) and Indra (Hindu) are powerful extravert gods also wielding thunder-bolts, while Vishnu, the preserver, represents the deeper wisdom of Jupiter.

Jupiter Keywords: Expansion, opportunity, justice, religion, preservation.

Saturn

Limitation is one of the principles of Saturn. It is the second largest planet and represents the limit of the solar system which can be seen with the naked eye. The planet is encircled by its rings, a girdle of icy rock dust and fragments—a symbolic containment appropriate to the planet's astrological principles. It takes around 2½ years to move through one sign and an average of 29½ years to complete the cycle of the zodiac. Saturn is one of the most important planets in the chart and yet one of the least understood. Mediaeval astrologers knew it as 'the great malefic' and indeed its principles can be seen in part as discipline, difficulty, limitation, responsibility and hard work. But Saturn is also the schoolteacher, one who seems to have a habit of setting examinations before the pupil has been taught the lesson. This appears harsh, but in reality the teachings are always available if the pupil searches for them. And if he searches diligently, and finds, then Saturn will be seen as a wise old man.

Each one of us has a soul which has chosen to wrestle with the difficulty of expressing spirit through the base material of a human body. Saturn represents that battleground; but the difficulties which may be initially experienced can be transmuted into qualities which, although serious, are none the less valuable—duty, control, conservation, stability and patience. However, there is a deeper side to Saturn which needs to be understood. The planet produces its effect by causing difficulty in the expression of the qualities of its sign, in the affairs of its house and in any planetary aspects. The difficulty is a feeling of underconfidence or even fear, an ill-defined discomfort which thereby limits the expression of sign, house and aspect. The individual either shrinks fearfully away or obliterates the negative feelings with overcompensating action. The discomfort cannot be ignored or swept under the carpet; it has to be accepted, confronted, understood and worked with so that the Saturn energy in the chart can be transformed into the strength which it promises.

The symbol ♄ is almost exactly the reverse of Jupiter's—reflecting the opposites of the two planets' principles. The cross of matter surmounts the half circle of soul, showing the discipline of the material world which the soul has chosen to experience.

In mythology, Saturn is Kronos, one of the many offspring of the union between Gaea, mother earth, and Ouranos, the star-filled sky, who was also her first son. Kronos, in league with his mother, castrated his half-brother father and then took over from his parents the supervision of the creation of the world. He swallowed each of his own children until he was tricked into swallowing a stone instead of the infant Zeus. The ancient prophecy was fulfilled when Kronos was overthrown by his son, forced to disgorge his other children and then banished into exile beyond the earth and the sea. There he became Lord of Time.

Saturn Keywords: Lessons to be learned, responsibility, duty, restriction, limitation.

Saturn and Jupiter are two great balancing forces, operating between the 'personal' faster-moving bodies and the outer planets, the slow-moving indicators of the collective. Jupiter can bring out the easier qualities of its sign and house placing while Saturn correspondingly produces seriousness and the growing pains which precede maturity. Saturn is the stronger, more noticeable influence of the two, both in the birth chart and especially by transit. But if the Saturn lessons are approached with consciousness and awareness, then the opportunities offered by Jupiter become more attainable.

The three outer planets, often referred to as 'higher octave', do not have such a personal influence as the seven inner planets, visible to the naked eye—their positions and mutual aspects are the same for all people born over long periods of time. Thus, they correlate with whole generations and with collective energies which affect society as a whole. But the way in which they integrate with the rest of the chart, paradoxically, has a strong influence. Their aspects to the personal planets and their possible angularity are particularly important. When this occurs the individual has a potential opportunity to experience and work with the collective energies, broadening his horizons and his field of influence. This could be by making some special contribution to society or perhaps in terms of personal evolution—but a conscious choice has to be made and the opportunity grasped. The personal planets blend more with the sign in which they are placed and allow the influence of that sign to manifest, whereas the outer planets, when strong in a chart, bring more of their own energy, direct and pure, through the chart into the character of the individual.

Uranus

The first of the outer planets, Uranus, was discovered in 1781—unexpectedly, because both astronomers and astrologers at that time believed there was nothing beyond Saturn. Visible only by telescope (except under unusual circumstances when it can be seen with the naked eye), Uranus spends about seven years in each sign and averages eighty-four years around the zodiac. Astronomically, the planet is eccentric, its axis of rotation tilting slightly from the horizontal, with the result that each pole alternatively experiences a hot and cold season of forty-two earth years each. Its discovery occurred around the time of the French Revolution, the Industrial Revolution and the war of American Independence; in astrology the principles of Uranus are revolutionary change, inventiveness, unexpected events and eccentricity. Many people ask if its discovery 'caused' the historical events of the time or whether astrologers decided on its influences because of what was happening in the world. The answer is neither; it is a case of synchronicity—the events were meaningfully coincidental. Mankind had evolved to the extent where he could take into his conscious awareness the energy of Uranus; at the same time, Uranian events were happening in the world all around him. The planet has always been there, but previously its influence was latent.

Revolution can grow from many roots—an anarchic desire to throw out the old regime, a petulant reaction against the establishment or a humanitarian ideal wanting to accelerate evolution. Uranus always looks to the future, intuitively sensing the possibilities, tuning into higher frequency communications. Indeed Uranus is often described as the higher octave of Mercury. Thomas Edison spoke of genius as '1 per cent inspiration and 99 per cent perspiration'—Uranus is that 1 per cent, the lightning flash often needing the conducting strip to bring it safely down to earth. The progressiveness of the planet also breeds eccentricity, deviation and rebelliousness, often expressing in highly charged, tense and unpredictable ways.

The symbol ♅ looks like a complex television aerial standing on a globe, but some interpretations merely point to the capital H of Herschel, the planet's discoverer. Perhaps these are escapes from the complexity of the make-up of the symbol itself. The cross of matter stands on the circle of spirit like the old Mars glyph, but two separated, outward-facing semi-circles are also attached. They may be two soul receptors feeding higher knowledge into the material cross elevated on spirit, or perhaps the soul half-circles are Janus-faced, suggesting a sacred doorway to new and unexpected levels of understanding. There is no single correct explanation, but meditation on the possibilities can lead to intuitive perception of deeper meaning.

As a god, Uranus was the starlit sky and received no cult in ancient Greece. But in the Rig-Veda the sky and the earth were known as the 'immortal couple' or 'the grandparents of the world'. Uranus' union with Gaea, his mother, not only formed the world, but also started the lineage of the Gods. Even his castrated genitals, falling into the sea caused Aphrodite to be born from the foam and the Furies rose from the ground where his blood was spilled.

Uranus Keywords: Sudden or unexpected change, inventiveness, originality, revolution.

Neptune

Neptune links us with mystical, other-wordly energies. It provides contact with intangibility in such a way that inspiration, spirituality, psychic powers and other extremes of sensitivity are made available to anyone who will release his bonds and allow the mysterious process to take place. Refinement is part of the process, but the balance is a fine one and it is easy for the rarified nature of Neptune's energies to become distorted and abused. Bring this intangibility into the everyday world and delusion, illusion, idealism and fantasy step in. Deceptively and enticingly it lulls us into Lethean reassurance—reminding us that Neptune also associates with drugs, alcohol, anaesthesia and escapism. Neptune is a pair of rose-coloured spectacles, a castle in the air or seven veils hiding a seductress who turns out to be only another phantom after the dance is over. Glamours of the material world can so easily be replaced by the often more insidious glamours of the spiritual world—but if the individual holds fast to the silver thread, like a sutratma leading through the mists, he will be able to connect with the higher refined reality promised by Neptune, universal love, the higher expression of Venus.

The planet was discovered in 1846 in circumstances of confusion and misunderstanding. Calculations were lost, communications were undated and on the clear night of the intended first sighting, cloud mysteriously appeared and obscured the sky. Neptune takes 165 years to travel the zodiac and spends about fourteen years in each sign. The history of popular music and the film industry (both ruled by Neptune) can be followed with the sign-change cycles.

In mythology, Neptunus was a sea-god with somewhat undefined duties, possibly because the Romans were comparatively uninterested in the maritime world. The Greeks recognized Poseidon as a powerful god ranking with Zeus, god of the heavens, and Hades, god of the underworld. This god of the waters was as irascible and licentious as all the other Olympians and not like the Neptune of astrology. Perhaps there are deeper myths still to be unveiled, but the symbology of Poseidon's realm remains. Water permeates everywhere; it takes on many forms—clear liquid, opaque foam, snow, ice, steam, cloud; it gives refreshment and life or it corrodes and wears down even the most solid rock, imperceptibly but inevitably. It washes and cleanses, but it can also drown.

The symbol Ψ has the appearnace of a sea-god's trident, but it can also be seen as the soul crucible with the cross of matter impaled but suspended from it.

Neptune Keywords: Refinement, inspiration, mysticism, deception, confusion.

Pluto

Pluto is the principle of transformation in the birth chart and it adds a deeper, more intense dimension to everything it touches. Where

Uranus is the breaking down and change of external structures, Pluto is change within—the earthquake, the volcano and the seed which can posses power enough to force its growth up, even perhaps eventually through concrete. Pluto promises the potential of the phoenix—that mythological bird which goes into the fire, dies and is born again, rising up with gorgeously renewed plumage. So there is also a connection with death, literally and symbolically. Before anything is born anew, the old must die and although the purging of the fire is not always easy, the regenerated substance becomes tempered steel. We must understand the nature of crisis. It is not the disaster it may seem, but an opportunity for new growth—in Chinese the character for 'crisis' is identical with the one for 'danger and opportunity'—an exciting challenge. Pluto is generally considered to be the higher expression of Mars, but some sources suggest Mercury. Certainly there is a link with more complex communication in that Pluto associates with psychology, exploring personal depths, the sewers of the unconscious. It also confronts death in all its forms—sexual orgasm of the two-backed beast, which the Elizabethans called 'the little death', death of the old personality and perhaps preparation for bodily death, shedding the soul's physical vehicle.

The planet was known about as early as 1905, the early years of depth psychology, but it remained hidden until its actual sighting in 1930. This was the time of the Nazis in Germany and crime syndicates in America. It was also when the means of unlocking immense power from the infinitesimal atom became a reality for mankind.

Pluto takes 248 years to move around the zodiac, but it can take anything from thirteen to thirty two years to move through a single sign. This is because of its unusually oblique orbit, which also causes it to come within the orbit of Neptune infrequently during its cycle of two and a half centuries. This happened at the end of 1978 and will remain so until March 1999. It is closest in 1989. Pluto will also be in its own sign of Scorpio from 1983—1995. The period from now until the end of the millenium will surely be an especially Plutonic period, a purging renewal for planet Earth and for the human race.

Two symbols are used for Pluto. ♇ is a monogram of the initials of both its discoverer Percival Lowell and its name (the name was apparently proposed by an eleven-year-old girl who was thinking of the Disney dog and not the god of the underworld. Strange are the ways of synchronicity). The other symbol ♀ suggests that spirit is hovering in the semi-circle of soul, over the cross of matter. It is almost as though a permanent atom of creation is undergoing an alchemical process, being heated by existence and experience in the material world.

All ancient cultures had their gods of the underworld (Orcus, Dis, Supai, Yawa, Osiris, Anubis, Hel) but it was for the Greeks that Pluto or Hades ruled. He abducted Persephone to his dark kingdom and often wore a helmet which made him invisible. But he was also the god of buried riches and mineral wealth and it was he who made the crops grow from beneath the ground.

Pluto Keywords: Transformation, regeneration, death and re-birth, elimination, the phoenix.

4.
THE SIGNS

The twelve equal divisions in space along the Zodiac wheel are like twelve different lenses of intricate complexity and variegated colour combinations. They tint the symbolic beam of energy shining from each planet, subtly modifying the pure planetary principles, embellishing and enhancing, but still allowing many different patterns to form, each different and yet each a valid expression of the planet/sign combination. For nothing is fixed in astrology; we are studying a subject which is one of the structures of the fluidity of life and there are many different ways of letting the planet/sign energies flow. Knowledge of those alternatives is psychological consciousness and this gives choice to the individual—and responsibility—as to how the energies may be used.

In moving towards an understanding of the twelve Zodiac lenses, we shall pass through various groupings which have certain interpretations in common—dualities, elements and qualities—and this will enable us to build our knowledge of the signs gradually but thoroughly.

Duality
The twelve signs can be divided most simply into two groups—positive/negative, masculine/feminine. The latter does not refer to sexual gender so much as archetypal masculine or feminine principles. Whether we are in a man's body or a woman's body, we all have the duality within us, the yin-yang, the active-passive, the alternating pulses of energy as in an electrical circuit. Part of our self-understanding and our ability to interpret an individual's horoscope is related to the extent to which we can balance and use these two opposite but complementary influences.

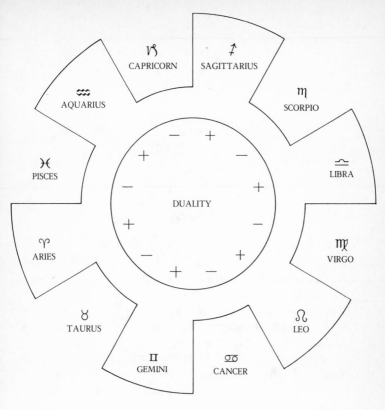

Figure 3.

The signs are alternately positive and negative, but the opposite signs have the same polarity. There is no implied criticism of the negative signs, nor is any supremacy of masculinity implied, for each needs the other. The six masculine signs do tend to be more positive, expressive and outgoing, while the six feminine signs lean towards receptiveness and containment. Yin receives, yang gives; between them the seed is fertilized and new life is created.

Elements

In astrology there are four elements—Fire, Earth, Air and Water—and it will be seen from the diagrams that their signs form triangulations within the Zodiac wheel. The Fire and Air signs have in common the fact that they are all yang/masculine and the Earth and Water signs yin/feminine.

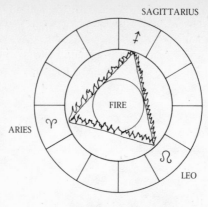

Figure 4.

The three Fire signs express their positive-active polarity through keeness and enthusiasm. Fiery indeed, they provide energy, warmth and that creative vision which can sometimes be seen in the flickering flames or hot embers on the hearth. But fire can also consume and reduce to ashes if it is allowed to get out of control. Excitement and a breadth of vision which encompasses all possibilities may have a certain glamour, but the fire signs are often lacking in that they may be unable to bring their visionary ideas into reality. The questing spirit is strong, sometimes to the extent that pause for a soft caress or a moment of gentleness is lost.

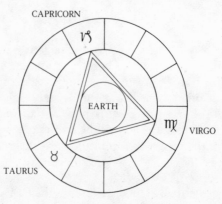

Figure 5.

The three Earth signs express the passive-yin polarity in practical groundedness and in caution. The well-rooted quality of this element bestows a natural ability for dealing sensibly and efficiently with the material world. Sadly, the Earth signs have acquired a dull, unadventurous image—unjustified, since all physical growth needs roots; and spirit needs matter for its manifestation. The adventure of the seed beneath the ground as it starts to grow is one of the most exciting and creative acts of nature.

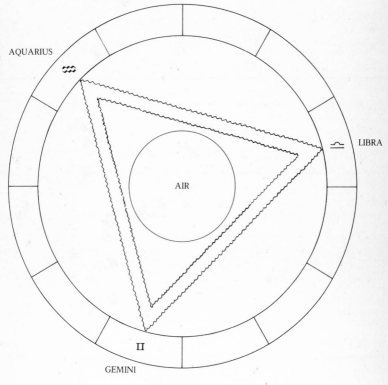

Figure 6.

The three Air signs express the positive-masculine polarity in their common desire to communicate, projecting outwards a mentally based energy. Air is an invisible linking medium common to all mankind, vital to life and carrier of *Prana*. The humanity of these three signs can indeed be a breath of fresh air and their intelligence and clear-headed ability to handle ideas, words and concepts is stimulating and refreshing. But a cooler breeze may also blow, for when the intellect reigns supreme, feeling and emotion are stilled by the rational mind and its code of finite reality.

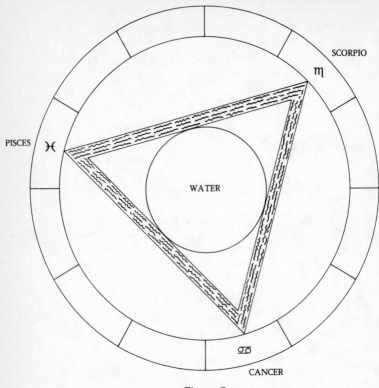

Figure 7.

The three Water signs express their negative-passive polarity in sensitivity and impressionability in the same way as a liquid needs a container and assumes its shape. Emotions ebb and flow like the tide; feelings are tranquil, rippled or stormy like the sea—but always many swirling currents exist in the depths. Such sensitivity bestows on the Water signs a compassion which eludes the other elements, but although water can cleanse and refresh it can also flood, dampen and drown. These signs can be unstable and spineless, so that sometimes initiative and purpose evaporate or seep away.

Qualities
The three qualities are Cardinal, Fixed and Mutable, forming crosses in the Zodiac wheel. Each is composed of one sign of each element.

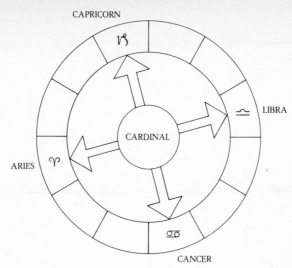

Figure 8.

Cardinal: The four Cardinals are the signs of initiative. They are well-suited to starting off any adventure, pioneering and expressing an outgoing creativity. But the powerful and independent will can become impatient and ruthless if self-motivation takes over completely.

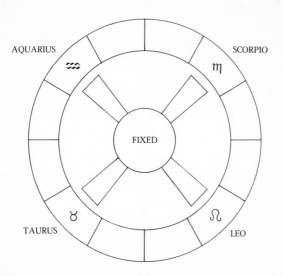

Figure 9.

Fixed: The word 'fixed' is an agreeably suitable description for these four signs. All have the common qualities of determination, loyalty and consistency. Once a person with the fixed signs strong in his chart has set sights on a goal there is little which will deter him; he is persistent and dependable. The less desirable expressions of this fixed energy are stubborness, intolerance and an inability to cope with or accept change when it occurs.

Mutable: Mutability is adaptability and flexibility. Where these signs are strong there is an ability to distribute and make use of energy—the Cardinal signs initiate and create, the Fixed signs consolidate and preserve, but the Mutable signs disseminate, either in constructive application or by frittering away. These signs can suffer from a lack of perserverance and purpose, bending with the wind whichever way it blows.

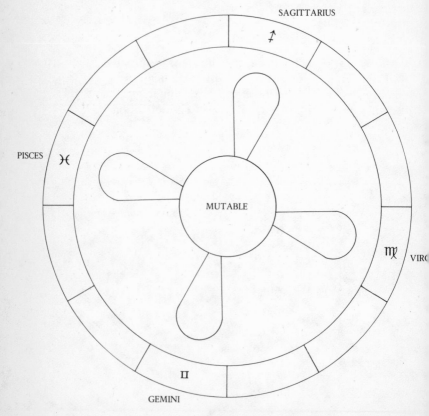

Figure 10.

People-Watching

At this point, 'people-watching' should be mentioned again. Human beings are inexplicable and yet predictable; irrational but lovable. They have happiness and fear, hopes and doubts, weaknesses and creative gifts. They are paradox incarnate and yet gods in potential. Watching these people—strangers, friends, loved ones and acquaintances (and of course yourself, for you are one of them—even though you hold a distorting mirror to yourself)—not only broadens basic astrological knowledge, but also strengthens the link between astrological theory and those real people in the world, struggling more or less successfully with their lives. Try this little game at any time—on a train, at a party, at work or wherever other human beings are gathered. Observe people for a few minutes and then decide whether they are predominantly Fire, Earth, Air or Water; Cardinal, Fixed or Mutable. This is better than 'guessing their sign' or translating the Element-Quality combination into a sign, for unless you can calculate their full chart you will not know whether you have sensed the Sun sign, Moon sign, ascendant or a sign with a stellium, a grouping of a number of other planets.

Having examined the sign groupings of two, three or four and taken note of the meanings of the Elements and the Qualities, we are now in a position to construct an interpretation of each sign. Onto this framework we can then build individual sign characteristics, ending up with a well-rounded understanding of the nature of our twelve zodiac lenses. Three groups of keywords are also given. These show the positive or natural expression, the less constructive or distorted expression and words which fall between the two. A keynote statement is also given to aid intuitive understanding of the sign.

ARIES: Positive—Cardinal—Fire ♈

The first sign of the zodiac is outgoing, initiatory and burning with enthusiasm—the combination of Cardinal and Fire is powerful and complementary and so there is a single-minded directness about everything attempted. The symbol is the ram. Tough and uncomplicated, this creature puts its head down and charges, butting persistently with the hard brow between the curved-back horns. The Aries temperament is the same once the decision has been made to start, nothing will get in his way. For those who wish to follow, he makes an impressive leader, brave and setting a fine example, but anyone who is not with him had best get out of his way. This ram can be a steamroller which flattens all obstacles. Indeed many battering rams are pictured as having a ram's head on the attacking end. The glyph shows the ram's horns, but it also suggests a representation of the first green shoots emerging from the seed in the ground, strong and full of expectation, thrusting their way up and out—symbolic springtime of any new venture. The symbol could also be seen as a wrought-iron spike, staking a claim in virgin land—'This is mine', says the pioneer.

Aries is the sign of individuality, the pure expression of self, and there is an uncomplicated quality in the way the sign's energies manifest. Courage comes naturally, because the purpose is single; difficulties are to be surmounted or destroyed, never avoided or given compromise. But warriors become restless in peace time and start looking for battles to fight and challenges to meet. It is easy for the 'self-ness' of Aries to express as selfishness, a simple philosophy of the centrality of the individual, naive and insensitive. Aries energy pulsates with power, but once the initiative has been taken, the enthusiasm often dwindles and the lack of sustained follow-up results in a petering out of the once proud venture.

Keynote:　　　'Primal energy expresses itself'.

Keywords:

Initiating	Simple directness	Aggressive/quarrelsome
Decisive	Self-interest	Impulsive
Leader and Pioneer	Assertive	Insensitive
Courageous		Impatient

TAURUS: Negative—Fixed—Earth ♉

The Earth element and Fixed quality makes Taurus like a strong oak tree, well-rooted in the ground. Dependable, immovable and practical, this sign will operate at its own speed and in its own time. The symbol is the bull, an animal which is strong, placid at times, but can be provoked into intense and powerful rage. The glyph is a pictogram of the bull's head—simple, solid and expressive. This second sign, like Aries, also has an uncomplicated quality, but here it associates with a back-to-nature simplicity, a living connection with the earth, fertility, all that grows and the beauty which has not been embellished with man's complexities. There is the sensuality of the Earth Goddess in Taurus. Such contact with the natural material world can bring a certain possessiveness to the sign—a desire for wealth, investment or money spent on objects of comfort, beauty or value.

Taurus people are usually artistic, directing their appreciation towards softer colours and textured surfaces; taking a piece of mother earth, clay or rock, and turning it into a thing of beauty would have a typical appeal. Taurean caution and conservatism come from the realisation that the natural order of life always achieves results in the end. Patience is a virtue and new-fangled devices create more problems than solutions—but these are philosophies which can lead to dullness and inactivity unless there is an awareness of the need for new growth upwards and not just roots growing downwards.

Keynote: 'My nourishment grows naturally from the earth'.

Keywords:

Loyal and Trustworthy	Nature-Loving	Possessive
Productive	Earthy and Sensual	Slow and Stolid
Artistic	Conservative	Covetous
Calm and Composed		Obstinate

GEMINI: Positive—Mutable—Air ♊

In simple terms, Gemini is adaptable (Mutable) and intellectual (Air). But this very combination creates its own complexity, a colourful weave of computer circuitry, brilliantly designed and fast in operation. The twins symbolize this sign and they stand for duality in every aspect. They are normally depicted as young boys, or a boy and a girl, and reflect the thirst for knowledge and experience that any inquisitive children crave. But they are highly-strung and impatient and want the knowledge immediately—and all of it—so the complexity of the sign is born not of a deep maturity but rather from a tangle of the twins' own making. The glyph similarly represents duality, but it can also symbolize the twin pillars of the gateway to knowledge.

Gemini has the skill to be involved with many different things at the same time, and, more than this, he needs such variety in order to live harmoniously and express his qualities. But the temptation is to do nothing in depth and, because he is clever enough to get away with it, superficiality becomes his method of achieving ever more variety, and amorality keeps conscience at bay. Communication in all its forms is essential—reading, writing and talking. Even into old age, the lightness, wit, and mental dexterity of youth are apparent—Gemini is the Peter Pan of the Zodiac.

Keynote: 'The mind communicates streams of information'.		
Keywords:		
Eloquent	Inquiring	Superficial
Versatile	Witty	Shifty and Amoral
Clear Thinker	Light and Cheerful	Lacks concentration
Alert		Excitable

CANCER: Negative—Cardinal—Water ♋

These qualities and element combinations create a paradox and there is a latent complexity in the fourth sign. Cardinality is out-going and purposeful, while Water is emotional and receptive. The glyph for the sign suggests the mother's breasts or the fertilization of the egg by the sperm. The sign itself is symbolized by the crab and we can learn much about the sign from this creature. Living in the corners of rocky pools and in the sand, it is timid and insecure in nature, and yet has pincer claws which can be used aggressively.

Cancer people need security and are as attached to their homes as a hermit crab is to its shell, but they will fight protectively if they or their family are threatened. The crab has a tough outer shell, but is softer and more vulnerable underneath. Many Cancerians hide or protect their emotions under a hard shell, particularly those men who feel a little insecure in their masculinity and are reticent about showing sensitivity. Crabby claws are brandished in a show of apparent aggression. There is a strong mothering instinct within this sign which can express with deeply caring emotions and sensitivity, but it can also smother and envelop. The crab moves sideways and this symbolizes the obliqueness and indirectness which the human Cancerian often uses as a way of solving the sign's active-passive paradox. In extreme cases this can become deviousness or emotional blackmail.

Keynote: 'Loved ones are nurtured protectively'.

Keywords:

Sympathetic	Maternal	Touchy
Protective	Family and Security	Devious
Understanding	Containing	Emotional Blackmailer
Kind and Caring		Grasping

LEO: Positive—Fixed—Fire ♌

Here fixity implies solidity and confidence, while Fire brings warmth and enthusiasm. The lion is known as the king of beasts and he displays his sovereignty with relaxed confidence. The glyph represents the flowing sweep of the lion's mane (or the rich long hair which many Leo people display), but it can also be seen as a line of energy emanating from a central source. Fixed Fire is like an eternal flame and Leo is gifted with an abundance of radiating power—benevolence, generosity, wisdom, creativity. Anyone with Leo strong in the chart knows he has the divine right of kings. He is happy to be the centre of attention and is self-assured in such circumstances. Some Leos look down on the lesser mortals around them, expect obedience and are discriminating in their associations. Other Leos are more benevolent rulers who love their subjects, bestowing bounty upon them and radiating a warmth which uplifts and inspires confidence.

Keynote: 'Solar energy shines out from my centre'.

Keywords:

Generous	Fearless	Arrogant
Self-Confident	Magnetic	Condescending
Warm	Easy-going	Vain
Creative		Imperious

The quality of Leonian creativity also comes from this radiation of energy. It is almost like an over-flowing which can be given out in abundance, a demi-God in a microcosm of Genesis—'my cup runneth over'. But creative temperamentality is always waiting in the wings, for demi-God can easily become prima donna. Above all, Leonians have total confidence in their individuality, in their right to be who they are and where they are—it seems that nothing can topple them from their thrones.

VIRGO: Negative—Mutable—Earth ♍

Adaptable (Mutable) and practical (Earth), Virgo is the sign of the good worker. People born with this sign strong are eager to be of service and are happiest when making their contribution with a good job well done. Often they will be workers behind the scenes, for they are modest and retiring and do not seek the limelight. Their practical concern with facts enables them to be expert and efficient in analysis, categorization and research. The sign is symbolized by the Virgin, the shy young girl, pure in mind and body. She is often shown as angelic, with wings, and is usually carrying a sheaf of corn denoting the fruitfulness of woman. The glyph is like a neat, intact M—meticulous, maiden, Mary. Virgo tends to be prudish and can feel guilty about sex—although if conforming in their environment means promiscuity, then they can approach it with matter-of-fact earnestness.

Virgo brings conscientiousness and virtuousness to the individual, but this often results in over-conformist behaviour. Perfection is a goal towards which all Virgoans strive—commendable at the right time and place, but over-exaggeration can lead to a critical attitude, finding fault with everything. Some Virgoans turn this in on themselves and become obsessed with worry and guilt. They generally have a concern for health and hygiene and are often involved with medicine, social services, diet or research.

Keynote: 'Service expresses through work'.

Keywords:

Dependable	Research	Critical
Hard worker	Prudent	Nervous and Apprehensive
Meticulous and Efficient	Differentiation	Prudish
Service		Calculating

LIBRA: Positive—Cardinal—Air ♎

The outgoing (Cardinal), intellectual (Air) qualities in Libra are often camouflaged by the symbol of the scales and its representation in the glyph—balance, harmony and equilibrium. This is the only inanimate symbol in the zodiac and yet relationship is one of the sign's main principles. Librans need another person to be in balance with and they seek harmony and beauty in everything, even to the extent of abhoring ugliness and squalor. Diplomacy is their forte and charm is natural to them. They find it easy to persuade other people to carry out tasks and little jobs for them, so that they sometimes seen indolent and languid. But if there is no willing servant around they readily do the job themselves. Libra's cardinality often expresses as a strong hand in the velvet glove. The harmony of relationship and of art and beauty is more of a concept or an ideal than a total involvement for a Libran. Certainly the picture will be painted, the art gallery appreciated and the partnership entered into, but all are done with composure rather than passion.

Whether in the role of lover, husband or wife, Librans show great affection and enjoy showing off their relationship in a social setting or as gracious host and hostess. Discussion, debate and negotiation are enjoyed as the scales move gently up and down. Some Librans find if difficult to make up their minds and their fence-sitting can result in a blandness of character, while others let the scales rock more violently in argument. They all have skills in strategic manoeuverings, the weighing and balancing before action, but often have difficulty in making a final decision.

Keynote: 'Equilibrium is achieved through relationship'.

Keywords:

Gracious and Sociable	Partnership	Indecisive
Impartial and Diplomatic	Strategist	Hedonistic
Artistic	Charmingly persuasive	Bland
Affectionate		Argumentative

SCORPIO: Negative—Fixed—Water ♏

Technically, the only way 'water' can be 'fixed' is when it is ice. Certainly the iceberg, like Scorpio, reveals little of itself, the greatest part being submerged and treacherous. People with Scorpio strong in the chart can be cold and hard, but there are other interpretations of Fixed-Water. Feeling and emotion are unbending here, determined and intense; great strength is implied—like a giant tidal wave is described as a wall of water. Scorpio used to be symbolized by a snake hiding dangerously in the grass, tempting Eve, or by a sacred creature eating its own tail as Ouroborus, symbol of oneness. The scorpion has a deadly poisonous sting in its tail to which it is virtually immune itself, but which it can mete out in calculated doses to quieten and paralyse a wriggling captive. And yet the mother scorpion caringly carries her young on her back instead of letting them fend for themselves after birth. Yet another symbol is the eagle or phoenix showing how Scorpio can rise up to the heights or be reborn.

Scorpio embodies extremes. It is the sign of heights and depths. Everything must be penetrated, examined and experienced, even down to the sewers and underground caverns of all aspects of human experience. Only when the excrement has been scrutinized does the eagle feel qualified to fly. There is passion and intense feeling in Scorpio—he will be a loyal friend or an avenging enemy, but always there is a strong idiosyncratic sense of justice. Use and abuse of power is a continuous struggle for Scorpians and the temptation is to try to control others—through sex, magic, hypnotism or just on day-to-day battlefields. Sexuality is a powerful energy, and Scorpio is especially immersed in it. The glyph for the sign has the sting in the tail, but it is also unashamedly phallic. 'M' is again the root of the glyph, but here representing money, another powerful energy associated with the sign.

Keynote: 'Extremes are purged in the fire and rise again'.

Keywords:

Penetrating	Secretive	Ruthless
Steadfast and tenacious	Passionate and intense	Suspicious and vindictive
Unflinching	Catharsis	Power-seeking
Deep regeneration		Destructive

SAGITTARIUS: Positive—Mutable—Fire ♐

Changeable, adaptable enthusiasm is the basic structure of Sagittarius. The sign is symbolized by the centaur shooting an arrow and the glyph represents that arrow as it leaves the bow. And like an arrow Sagittarian enthusiasm is directed towards the far horizons and the wide-open spaces. There is a restlessness about people born with this sign strong and they love sport, physical activity, riding and travel. They are independent and nomadic, because they always need involvement with the distant goal—the problems of the immediate environment do not interest them. If they take a tumble in life it is often because they have not attended to some dull, everyday obstacle at their feet, being too concerned with the excitement of a wider, more distant objective. In the same way, many Sagittarians are also physically clumsy. Certainly they have an irresponsible streak, but their optimism and extrovert enthusiasm is infectious, and their sincerity and directness can be a tonic—until it turns into tactlessness, excessive heartiness, exaggeration and insensitivity.

'Mental travel' takes the Sagittarian into the realms of philosophy, metaphysics and religion. Here the quest is for knowledge and wisdom, but the same enthusiasm accompanies it. In excess this becomes preaching and even religious fanaticism. The cause is just, but Sagittarian insensitivity and even a tendency towards amorality clouds any sense of proportion.

Keynote: 'The arrow speeds on its quest to the far horizon'.

Keywords:

Enthusiastic and jovial	Independent	Exaggeration
Optimistic	Traveller	Blunt and boisterous
Sincere	Frank and open	Hypocritical
Teacher of Wisdom		Rash and irresponsible

CAPRICORN: Negative—Cardinal—Earth ♑ ♑

Earth brings practicality and caution, while cardinality presents initiative and out-going activity. Thus there is a determined patience about Capricorn, the knowledge that achievement will come about in the fullness of time. The symbol is the goat, painstakingly climbing upwards towards the peak of his ambition. But often a goat with a sea creature's tail is used, symbolizing the deeper potential in the sign. This 'Mer-Goat' can still negotiate the craggy mountain, but it has the collective wisdom and sensitivity of the waters which it is also able to use. This is the only sign with two glyphs, both having the feeling of an austere bonyness or a twisted goat's horn. There is the strength and permanence that exists in the hard wood of a mature climbing plant, but both glyphs also include a suggestion of the Mer-goat's tail.

People with Capricorn strong in their charts will always be involved with the material world—building achieving and organizing. Material success is important and is usually achieved, but sometimes at the expense of worshipping the god Mammon. Wealth and status are needed so that the world can see the achievements, but in the pathway towards this goal the over-serious, grasping and rigidly authoriatarian side of Capricorn can manifest. The structure which is built so skillfully becomes a prison. But Capricorn can rise above this and become that vital link between spirit and matter. He can ground the vision to by using the material world for the wider good rather than being used by it, allowing the vision to become obscured. The latter temptation is ever present, but so also is the potential for reaching the highest of the peaks.

Keynote: 'With discipline the peak is reached and experienced'.

Keywords:

Sense of responsibility	Executive	Rigid and demanding
Organizer and builder	Ambitious	Authoritarian
Patient	Dignified	Avaricous
Spirit in matter		Gloomy and limited

AQUARIUS: Positive—Fixed—Air ♒

A determined (Fixed) intellectual (Air) approach characterizes Aquarius. People with this sign strong usually appear to have an above average intelligence, enhanced by an inventive and forward-looking attitude—scientists, inventors and other progressive thinkers, for example. Air sign coolness expresses here as detachment and lack of deep personal involvement, which allows the Aquarian to indulge his eccentricities without batting an eyelid. In fact he does not see himself as eccentric, merely a little ahead of his time and misunderstood by the less aware members of the human race. Some Aquarians become revolutionaries or drop-outs if misunderstood, for it is the broad ideals which matter and society is to blame if they are rejected. The group is more important to an Aquarian than the individual and friendship comes more naturally than deep personal involvement. Often when a love relationship is causing difficulty, the response will be to cut off and defend with cool detachment rather than become involved with each other's feelings. Humanity, society, the starving masses and the oppressed minorities are all given preference over any one individual, and therefore the Aquarian is a dedicated champion of the cause, face-upturned towards his ideals and seeking the truth. The glyph represents lines of communication and electric energy in the air; the symbol is the man pouring out the water of knowledge for humanity.

Keynote: 'New ideals are presented to humanity'.

Keywords:

Truth-seeker	Scientist and inventor	Cool and detached
Humanitarian	Brotherhood and equality	Eccentric
Friendly and gregarious	Progressive	Rebellious drop-out
Co-operative		Sceptical

PISCES: Negative—Mutable—Water ♓

Changeable (Mutable) and feeling (Water), Pisces is the most sensitive and other-worldly of all the signs. Water itself is changeable, adaptable and impressionable, taking on the shape of whatever container surrounds it. Pisces is symbolized by the fishes, swimming in the water, but tied together and pointing in opposite directions. Sometimes they swim in confusion, sometimes they strain against the tension of man as God and man as man. The glyph reflects this also, the two outward-facing semi-circles held together by one joining line. The early Christians used the fish as their symbol, Jesus being known as Ikthos, the fish. He preached the Piscean doctrine of love and self-sacrifice.

The person with Pisces strong in the chart is sensitive to the extent of almost having no boundaries—he will merge with the environment like a sponge breathes water, psychically aware of other levels of existence, but also vulnerable to the harsher aspects of earthly existence. This gives opportunity for extremes of spiritual and mystical experience, but also makes the Piscean prone to hurt and to confusion, deception and illusion. Escapism is necessary too, but preferably channelled into inspirational areas, music and art, avoiding the seductive appeal of drink, drugs and dissipation. Self-sacrifice is strong in Pisces, giving the ability to be accepting of life and to allow a oneness with all creation—'not my will, but thine be done'. But he can also be easily put upon by a tale of hardship which evokes his sympathy.

Keynote: 'The self is sacrificed in the waters of redemption'.

Keywords:

Compassion and sensitivity	Idealistic	Confusion
Grasps intangibles	Self-sacrificing	Masochistic and submissive
Unselfish	Imaginative	Lacks individuality
Spiritual and mystical		Dreamy

5.
MORE ABOUT THE SIGNS

Planetary Rulerships

Each sign is said to have a 'ruling planet'. This means that there is a synchronous quality or sameness between certain planets and certain signs and it is important to be familiar with these relationships. A planet can never in any way replace a sign, or vice versa, but a planet which is strongly placed in a chart (close to the ascendant for example) will bring to the person's character the qualities of the sign which it rules, almost as much as qualities of the planet itself. Active awareness of this sort of correlation is one of the factors in chart interpretation which will help synthesis to grow out of analysis.

Figure 11 shows the rulerships and is also a useful way of remembering them. The Sun and the Moon rule the adjacent signs Leo and Cancer respectively. Then the planets, in astronomical

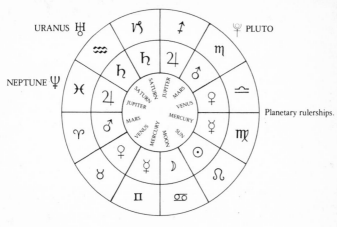

Figure 11.

order from the Sun to Saturn rule two signs each working outwards from Cancer and Leo. These rulerships date back far beyond the invention of the telescope. When the three outer planets (Uranus, Neptune and Pluto) were discovered they were assigned rulership of one of the Saturn, Jupiter and Mars ruled signs respectively. Mercury and Venus are still sole rulers of two signs each, but many astrologers believe that there are two more planets still to be discovered so that at some point in the future there will be no dual rulerships.

Leo—Sun: The power and life-giving energy of the Sun correlates with the shining benevolence and creativity of Leo. The firey Sun is 'fixed' at the centre of our solar system, a sovereign on his throne sending out not only warmth and radiation, but a gravitational pull strong enough to hold the planets in their orbits around him.

Cancer—Moon: Feminine responsiveness and feeling, as symbolized by the Moon, are in harmony with the caring and protectiveness of Cancer. Maternal instinct and nurturing breast is always present, but the sign also embodies the cyclic mysteries of the feminine, ever-changing and flowing.

Gemini—Mercury, Virgo—Mercury: Two mutable signs each allow different expression of the same principle of communication. Gemini communicates in the air element—the spoken word, the written word and the ideas and thoughts that those words provoke. Virgo provides grounding and structure for Mercury's communication—libraries, hospital records and maps, any form of analysis, categorization and research.

Taurus—Venus, Libra—Venus: The principle of harmony, relationship and art correlates with Taurus simply and naturally. To a Taurean, a tree is a work of art which responds to being touched; home-grown, home-cooked food is harmonious nourishment and a beautiful way of experiencing the involvement of relationship is making love on spring-time grass in the open air. The Venus element in Libra expresses with aesthetic balance. Works of art beautify the surroundings; relationship is the equilibrium of two people in love; harmony is the absence of ugliness and strife.

Aries—Mars, Scorpio—Mars: The masculine energy of Mars, its drive, activity and sexuality confirms the assertiveness of Aries and the power of Scorpio. Aries is the sign of warrior, gladiator and lone ranger—fighting as an individual, winning the spurs of his manhood. Scorpio fights for different reasons—to achieve power, to take revenge, to see justice done or solely to destroy. Scorpio acts secretly—a knife in the shadows or passionate coupling under cover of darkness.

Sagittarius—Jupiter, Pisces—Jupiter: Jupiter's expansiveness and its creation of opportunity emphasises the enthusiasm of Sagittarius. Sport is enjoyment, travel broadens the mind, religion and philosophy lead the searcher towards his goal. The Piscean demonstrates Jupiter's energy just as generously but less boisterously. He opens his arms and his heart with love for his fellow-men; sacrifice of the self is no real loss—it only makes more room for God to grow within.

Capricorn—Saturn, Aquarius—Saturn: The discipline and control of Chronos, God of Time, reflect in the austerity, seriousness and patience of Capricorn. Rome was not built in a day, life is hard and lessons must be learned. Aquarians show Saturnian traits slightly differently in their potential to ground their progressive ideals and their inventive thoughts. Science may seem to be the spearhead of technological progress, but it can nevertheless be remarkably conservative and structured in its approach to knowledge.

There is also a harsher side to Aquarius which will force its ideals upon people. Such an Aquarian might be advocate of a state system set up for the common good but which easily develops into a totalitarianism which suffocates the individual. Or he might make an unbending demand that humanity accepts the vision of the New Age—*his* vision, automatically assumed to be right for everyone.

Aquarius—Uranus: The discovery of Uranus released Aquarius from the more restrictive aspect of Saturn rulership. Symbolically, the flash of genius arrived and scientific breakthrough became reality. Progress knows no conventions in Aquarius and the possibilities for the human race are now limitless, beyond even the most bizarre of previous dreams. Aquarians look to the future and the utopian world they strive for seems to be within their grasp. If evolution moves too slowly, then revolution may be needed to cut away the dead wood and the crystalized growth of old structures and out-of-date systems.

Pisces—Neptune: The new ruler of Pisces reveals a deeper more spiritual aspect of the sign. Pisceans are able to transcend day-to-day earthly bonds and reach a mystical attunement with the oneness of the Creator. But the penalty they pay for this privilege is difficulty in handling the material world, in organizing their lives and in separating psychic reality from earthly reality. And even when they have achieved this separation they still have the problem of differentiating between levels of psychic reality—receiving inspiration or falling prey to illusion.

Scorpio—Pluto: Mars points to the manifesting power of Scorpio, but Pluto helps us to understand its hidden power. If a person with Scorpio strong in his chart is to release the phoenix potential from his inner being, he must search in Pluto's underworld kingdom, for it is from here that transformation will start. Like the nigredo, the blackening in the alchemical process, or like 'the dark night of the soul', it is from confrontation with shadow that the third creative force breaks through. Pluto rules death and the continuous inner wrestling of Scorpio is like a series of deaths, each one followed by a rebirth. Scorpio can reach the power of the atom and has the choice to use it either destructively in a nuclear explosion or constructively as an atomic generator of energy.

The Signs in Sequence
The zodiac wheel can be observed as a dynamic cyclic process from which we can learn more about each sign by examining them in sequence. This is not intended to have any literal interpretative meaning, but rather to develop broader understanding of the signs and further encourage the ability to synthesize the separate interpretative factors of the chart. The signs can be divided into three sequential groupings—Elemental (Aries—Cancer), Individual (Leo—Scorpio), Universal (Sagittarius—Pisces), and each can be seen as a sub-cycle within the zodiac.

Aries—Cancer: The Aries seed of energy is planted and the first shoots push proudly and individually into the open. Hope, anticipation and enthusiasm provide the motive power and the wheel begins to turn. But the initial efforts of an Arian often dry up and interest wanes, so that the consolidating power of Taurus is needed to maintain the movement. Solid, grounded and dependable, the Taurean is well-fitted to keep the shoulder to the wheel. Where Aries provides an independent beginning, Taurus can produce something constructive which has some material worth. The problem comes when the creation, now something of value, is retained as a possession and thereby limited in its potential. The Taurean can learn much about the use of possessions from the next sign. Gemini knows about communication in all its forms and will disseminate and put to use all that Aries started and Taurus built. But there is an impersonal theorising, an over-clever quality in the Gemini method of utilization—it needs the feeling quality of Cancer to bring constructive, human use to the pattern. The now modified Aries energy is given stability and security by Cancer, perhaps based in a family group, protected and nourished by the values of tradition and the past.

Leo—Scorpio: The cycle of the first four signs completes a simple progression which ends in comfortable security. But the process of growth is never that cosy and the Cancerian has to learn that the nourishing, insulated group so dear to that sign can and should become a breeding culture for Leo activity. Here the individual learns self-expression, confident and out-going, and it is from this strong personal centre that the Leonian individual lights the spark of new creation. But, in its exuberance, the now strongly burning energy needs the careful channelling of Virgo to guide it into practical use and service. Once this has been achieved, however, Libran influence is required to prevent too much discrimination and categorization. Efficiency needs to be humanized and the Libran energy achieves this by introducing the concept of harmony, relationship, art and beauty. Balance and the appreciation of human values and of other people's needs soften the austerity of Virgo. And then Scorpio takes the process one step further. If Libran equilibrium is unmodified and left to its own devices, it can take on a Garden of Eden quality which has little to do with real life—what was humanity becomes a beautiful reproduction, coolly appreciated as if it were on display in an art gallery. Scorpio plunges this Libran/Virgo perfection into the swirling subterranean currents of human emotions. It upsets the balance and allows no peace, forcing even that which was deeply hidden to be confronted. What was a virgin marriage is initiated into the extremes of sexual involvement, from which a new consciousness is born.

Sagittarius—Pisces: The cycle of the four individual signs, Leo to Scorpio, deals with interpersonal dynamics. The new-born child growing from that cycle needs purpose and direction if it is to escape from the Scorpio maelstrom, which can be a vicious spiral easily able to distort the deep feelings and involvements which have been experienced. Sagittarius provides the vision of new horizons and higher purpose which is needed to lift the process up into the universal phase within the zodiac. But the extreme transition from the depths to the heights can be intoxicating. Wisdom is not guaranteed to be permanent and the Sagittarian's enthusiasm can lead to idealism or even fantaticism, so the presence of Capricorn is very necessary to bring structured purpose and direction. The Sagittarian knows where he wants to go and what goal he wants to achieve, but so often he has no idea of how to achieve it—how to bring firey spirit into material manifestation. Although the Capricornian person is able to do this using his formal skills to ground the energy, he too can become intoxicated in his own way on the centaur's wine, seeking even greater achievement (for its own sake), increasing his authority and creating dogma. The following sign, Aquarius, can loosen this cold grasp and make Capricorn's achievements available to mankind by pouring out the waters of knowledge for all people to quench their thirst. The Aquarian will stand up for human rights and break down the Capricornian's structure if it becomes too rigid. He is champion of society and is always ready to give support to a new cause, but the broadness of his objectives can lead to an impersonal, almost android-like attitude.

He needs compassion and he needs, in the end, to be able to release his control mechanisms so that a natural flow takes place, ending with a oneness with the creator. Society, groups, causes, are only temporary vehicles for individual members of the human race to use in their cyclic journey back to the source of all being. Pisces fulfils this need, representing the final dissolution of identity. In such mystical realms it is possible for disorientation to occur; the rebel Aquarian drop-out can unite with the Piscean misfit and the electricity is lost in a damp short-circuit. But the potential of Pisces is a union with the origin of creation—losing the little self in order to find the true Self. The ultimate sacrifice is achieved and yet the complete cycle starts again, for there is always the new Aries beginning which will follow, like the first primordial creatures crawling out of the sea onto the land for another journey of evolution—seed, growth, experience, application and unification.

The Signs in Polarity

The polarities should not be seen as two signs in conflict with each other—their positive expression is to create a natural balance and equilibrium. Each sign has something to learn from its opposite, but also has a contribution to make towards the other sign's more evolved expression.

Aries—Libra: Positive and Cardinal, this polarity in some ways epitomises the battle of the sexes. Venus seeks union, Mars acts independently and fights, but as with relationships between man and woman, each needs the other. The tough individuality of Aries needs to learn the balance and co-operation offered by Libra. Self-orientation and the desire for freedom can mellow through the experience of the need for compromise in a relationship with another person. But Libra's social involvement and the feeling of loss that exists without the 'other half' of the partnership may lead to vacillation and dependence. Libra is gently strengthened if it can develop the qualities of initiative and single-mindedness characterized by its opposite.

Taurus—Scorpio: This polarity is concerned with desire, feeling and possessions. It is a Venus Mars relationship, soft feminine and hard masculine, but it is also Venus Pluto, harmony and implosion. Taurus expresses with an earthly simplicity, but Scorpio can teach it the value of the deeper experience—enjoyment and creativity become passion; uncomplicated holding may become an aspect of power and reproduction is only one small part of the complexities of sexuality. But for all this seeming evolution, Scorpio's intense whirlpool has much to learn from Taurus—stability, patience and natural growth, like the peacefully regular cycles of the seasons.

Gemini—Sagittarius: Gemini is preoccupied with knowledge. Facts are a fascination and the individual wants to know how they fit into the scheme of things. Sagittarius can bring a height of wisdom to this vast storehouse of often indiscriminately collected information, allowing the whole broad picture to be seen clearly and understood intuitively. Jupiter expands the quotidian of Mercury, and yet Gemini can conversely help Sagittarius by bringing the ideals, the vision and the dogmas down into the real, practical world. Communication is a two-ended process and Gemini can sift the information so that it is easily assimilated by other members of the human race.

Cancer—Capricorn: This Water-Earth polarity compares the
fluctuating femininity of the Moon with the rigid structure of
Saturn. Both signs have the initiating power of cardinality, but with
their negative-yin-receptivity both signs are also paradoxes. Cancer
knows the emotional value of family, tradition and roots, but there
is a lack of practical ambition. The individual may also be easily
influenced, sensitive to another's needs, and may only indirectly
achieve his aims. Capricorn shows the attitude needed to succeed in
the world and demonstrates how to build something solid and of
lasting value, but often this is achieved at the expense of human
feeling. Caring, sympathy and kindness are lost in the discipline
and authority of the efficient organisation, but Capricorn's
structure can be softened by lunar Cancer's influence.

Leo-Aquarius: The balance of this polarity is between the artist
and the scientist, the individual and the group, the autocrat and the
democrat. Leo is self-centred and radiates self-confidence like the
Sun radiates warmth, while the pure Aquarian is only one cog in a
vast operating system, albeit a crucial component. The extreme of
the personality cult of Leo creates an arrogant dictator who may
become oblivious to the existence of his subjects as anything other
than exploitable serfs. Aquarius looks after the rights of men either
with   a   Saturn-like   legislature   or   by   progressive   Uranian
innovations, upholding the cause and the ideals. But the Aquarian
can so easily lose his personal identity by over-emphasizing the
needs of the group and he must look towards the creative
individuality of Leo for support.

Virgo—Pisces: This is the polarity of service. Virgo represents
meticulous, hard-working efficiency and Pisces demonstrates
compassionate, generous self-sacrifice. Both have much to offer the
world, but also much to teach the opposite sign. Virgo can reduce
everything to statistical analysis, dissecting the whole and using
each part economically so as to achieve maximum effectiveness.
The expression of Mercury needs the wider, more generous
application of Jupiter or the sensitivity of Neptune. Pisces shows
that hard work and service are enriched by humanitarian
application and spiritual inspiration. But if the Piscean does not
seek to learn from the Virgo opposite, then ideals become merely
castles in the air and sense of purpose is diluted by indiscriminate
compassion and sacrifice.

6.
THE HOUSES

The zodiac can be thought of as a great wheel surrounding the Earth along whose rim the planets move. It is almost as if this wheel is fixed against the backdrop of the heavens, with the signs, the twelve sections of that wheel, marked along the circumference. The astrological houses are like the spokes of a moving wheel, superimposed on the greater wheel, rotating once every twenty-four hours as a result of the daily revolution of the earth. The cusp (or leading edge) of the first house is known as the Ascendant and is the true horizon of an individual observer on Earth. Thus the Ascendant or rising degree is different at any given moment for observers in different parts of the world and it also changes as time passes. Indeed all the signs of the zodiac are on the Ascendant at some during every twenty-four-hour period. If the Sun is in Gemini on a given day, then at dawn when the Sun rises, Gemini will also be rising. At dusk on that day when the Sun sets, Gemini will also be setting and the opposite sign, Sagittarius, will be on the Ascendant.

The twelve divisions of the houses are always counted anti-clockwise from the Ascendant and the sizes of the houses can vary. It is not necessary in this book to explain the astronomical basis of the houses, but it is important to realize that there are a great number of different possible house systems, each one having its dedicated following. This means that planets can move from one house to another in the same chart using different house systems. These facts are a source of unease for the rationally-minded student who will ask, quite logically: 'Which is the *right* house system?' The infuriating answer is that they all can be, but that different astrologers find it easier to work with different systems. It is suggested that the student picks one system to start with, later experimenting with a number of them and then deciding which one he favours. Some astrologers even draw up all their charts using more than one house system.

However, the following remarks may help both understanding and acceptance of the house division problem. The simplest system is Equal House, where all the houses are 30° in size, and there is no concern with any of the complex astrological and philosophical arguments surrounding the other systems. But the Midheaven, the culminating degree of the zodiac, is also an important point on the chart and the Equal Houses system allows it to fall where it will. All the other conventional house systems use the Midheaven (M.C.) as the cusp of the tenth house and since the M.C. is usually not exactly 90° from the Ascendant, this means that the intermediate houses are either greater or smaller than 30° in size. These quadrant house systems, as they are known, include Placidus, Campanus, Koch and Topocentric; in very simple terms, the various astronomical calculations are based on either divisions in space or elapses of time. Because astrology is so intimately involved with time, I prefer the time-based systems and, of them, Placidus tables are the most readily available. But whatever system is used, there is nearly always going to be doubt in the chart because so few people know their birth time accurately. This means that the Ascendant may be, say, 5°-10° earlier or later and corresponding differences will exist on the intermediate house cusps.

It is generally accepted that planets in the early degrees of a house have the strongest house influence and that planets towards the end of a house can be additionally interpreted as being in the following house. But a more cynical view is that a planet in the middle of a house is the only position one can be sure of, what with uncertain birth times and so many different house systems! Indeed, Winter-born Eskimos perhaps have no Ascendant at all, since for many months of the year the sun remains below the horizon.

All of which serves to remind us when we are interpreting the chart that, although we are fortunate to have this cosmic science of astrology available to us, there are still many unresolved areas. We must always be seeking to learn more, to find answers to the questions and to increase our knowledge. But we must also remember that there is much that is unknowable. I favour approaching our subject with reverence and humility, for we are guilty of hubris is we think we can know all the answers.

The houses themselves represent areas of life or fields of experience which receive a particular focus from the planets in that house. In any chart there will always be houses which have no planets. This does not mean that the affairs of that house will be non-existent for the individual, rather that there will be no major emphasis in that area. As far as that house is concerned, the person can almost 'take it or leave it'. But if one wants to know more about the affairs of that house the placing of the house's ruling planet will assist the interpretation. The ruler is the planet which rules the sign on the cusp of the house or which is otherwise associated with that house—and it is quite possible for a house to have more than one ruler. (Figure 12, p. 62 explains this more clearly.)

For example, if the house of marriage is empty is does not mean that the person will not be married, nor that they will necessarily have especial happiness or difficulty in close personal relationships, but the suggestion is rather that the soul perhaps wanted to focus more on other areas of life in this incarnation.

The meaning of the houses are as follows:

1st House: The individual sense of identity. Self-image. Personal independence. Initiative. The physical body.

2nd House: Money. Financial security. Personal possessions. Reward for effort. Sense of value. 'Emotional possessions' —feelings.

3rd House: Communication with the immediate environment —conversation, letters, telephone, publications. Mental interests. Education. Journeys of short duaration. Brothers and sisters. Neighbours.

4th House: Home or base. Family. Sense of security. Ancestral and racial roots. Psychological conditioning. Parents (usually the father). The end of life.

5th House: Creative self-expression. Artistic pursuits. Enjoyable activities and recreation. Talents. Love and romance. Children. Risks, speculation and gambling.

6th House: Work—daily tasks, employment, duties. Service. Employees and dependents. Health, hygiene and diet. Domestic pets.

7th House: Close personal relationships. Cooperative involvement. Marriage. Business partners. Enemies. Harmony and conflict.

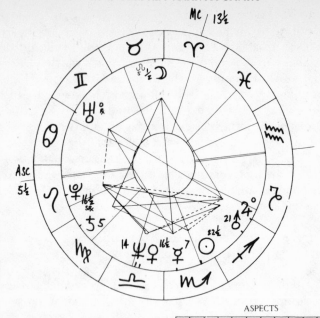

ASPECTS

The ascendant is Leo therefore the chart ruler and the first house ruler is the Sun. Some houses have more than one ruler. The fifth house has Scorpio on the cusp and is ruled by Pluto and Mars, but Sagittarius is said to be 'intercepted' in the fifth house and therefore Jupiter is also a ruler. Saturn, ruler of Capricorn at the end of the house, may also have an influence on this house. Where a house cusp is, for example, 29° Aries (not shown on Prince Charles' chart), technically the house ruler is Mars, the ruler of that sign, but the subsequent sign, Taurus, will have an additional strong connection with the house and Venus will be a ruler also.

Thus, the house rulers are as follows:

1. Sun
2. Sun, (Mercury)
3. Mercury, (Venus)
4. Venus, (Pluto, Mars)
5. Pluto, Mars, Jupiter, (Saturn?)
6. Saturn, (Uranus?)
7. Uranus, Saturn
8. Uranus, Saturn, (Neptune, Jupiter)
9. Neptune, Jupiter, (Mars)
10. Mars, (Venus)
11. Venus, Mercury, (Moon?)
12. Moon, (Sun?)

Figure 12. The chart of Prince Charles (with Placidus house cusps) to illustrate house rulerships and aspects.

8th House: Deeper involvement with others. Sex. Other people's emotions. Other people's possessions. Legacies. Investment, insurance and business corporations. Birth, death and re-birth. Research. Depth psychology.

9th House: Travel and foreign countries. Expanded consciousness. Further education and deeper studies. Philosophy and religion. Prophecy. Law, advertising and publicity.

10th House: Sense of worldly achievement. Profession and career. Status and fame. Social standing and social contribution. Parents (usually the mother).

11th House: Friends and associates. Hopes and wishes. Broad objectives and motivation. Ideals and altruistic interests. Groups and societies.

12th House: Secluded and sacrificial service. Mysticism and psychism. Contemplation and inner nourishment. Karmic lessons. Deep sorrows. Hidden relationships. Repressions and neuroses. Institutions—hospitals, prisons and asylums.

The houses can be divided into three groupings of four houses each—Angular, Succedent and Cadent. An examination of these groupings helps our understanding of the houses and is also a convenient opportunity to look at the house polarities.

Angular
The angular houses (1, 4, 7 and 10) represent those areas of life where we actively express ourselves and have important self-identification. Character energy cannot remain passive in these houses. The angular houses correspond to the cardinal signs.

1st and 7th House: These houses show the person's individual self-image and how he relates in close contact with other people. In any personal relationship (7th House) an individual will be seeking qualities (consciously or unconsciously) which will complement his personality (1st House) or which are needed to fill some psychological gap in his character. The signs and planets connected with these houses will show what these needs are.

4th and 10th House: The fourth house represents inward facing activity and motivational drives resulting from home life and upbringing, whilst the tenth house is the outward manifestation of them. Career, achievement and what the world remembers a person for (10th House) are all outward expressions of independence and maturity, but they also have a strong link with upbringing and the home (4th House). These two houses represent the parents who are always psychologically and emotionally important to every individual. They can be anything from encouraging, helping and non-interfering to restricting and manipulative. (See Chapter 9) Planets in these houses, the signs on the cusps and their rulers will indicate the importance of home and career and the balance between the two.

Succedent

The succedent houses (2, 5, 8 and 11) show the personal and material resources of the individual and how he maintains, conserves and develops his energies. There is a quality of stability about the succedent houses; planets and signs involved with them indicate practical utilization of personal energies. These houses correspond to the fixed signs.

2nd and 8th House: The two houses show personal finance and possessions and the way in which the individual relates with other people's possessions. The second house indicates simple personal values, but the much more complex eighth house shows how these values are projected out, materially, emotionally and psychologically.

5th and 11th House: The fifth house is where a person consolidates and expresses his individuality through various creative pleasures, but the eleventh house is a less personal, more widely varying expression of individuality. It indicates altruistic attitudes and activities, friendships, social connections and broad motivations, whilst the opposite fifth house is much more individually centred.

Cadent

The cadent houses (3, 6, 9 and 12) show how and where energy will be distributed by the individual. Planets connected with these houses will interact with the environment and with people contacted in daily life. There is an adaptable transitional quality about these houses and they correspond to the Mutable signs.

3rd and 9th House: Local travel—long distance travel; early education—further education; direct communication and information—deeper philosophies and metaphysics; the ninth house seems an extension of the third in every way. But the two balance each other, because the practical immediacy of communication indicated by the third house is needed if the more abstruse ninth house ideas are to be understood.

6th and 12th House: The work and service represented by the sixth house is taken into deeper, wider and more complex areas by the affairs of the twelfth house. The former house shows work for its own sake, practical and useful, whereas the latter concentrates more on the concept of service for the collective good; the individual ego is allowed to retire to a subordinate role.

Ascendant, Midheaven and the Angles

The cusps of the angular houses in any quadrant house system are known as 'the angles' and are always powerful and important points on the chart. Any planet close to an angle is increased in strength and its interpretation in the chart is correspondingly more important, referring particularly to the angular house involved. The Ascendant, the cusp of the first house, is the most important of the four angles, since it is the strongest part of the most individual house in the chart. This is the outer personality, the way in which we meet the immediate environment and it is that part of our character which a new acquaintance is likely to be first aware of. Thus the sign on the Ascendant, the rising sign, has as much weight in the chart as the Sun sign, although the expression of that sign will be slightly more extroverted than if it were the Sun sign. Any planet on or near the Ascendant (and to a lesser extent in the first house) will colour the personality as represented by the rising sign. For example a charming, diplomatic, well-balanced Libra rising individual, will have an additional assertive edge given to his personality if Mars is on the Ascendant. Because Mars rules Aries, it is almost as if he has an Aries Ascendant as well as Libra. This concept of correspondences which runs throughout astrology is a useful aid to synthesizing chart interpretation and a table is given at the end of this section to help the student recognize the correspondences.

The Midheaven (M.C.) is not usually given the same weight of consideration as the Ascendant, but it is important to include it in the interpretation of the chart. If the Ascendant is the outer part of the individual's personal character, then the M.C. is his public face, his social mask and how he meets the wider environment.

Both the Ascendant and M.C. should be considered not only as individual points but also axes; as discussed in the section on angular houses, both have a direct relationship with their opposites. The Ascendant is the individual alone; the Descendant is his close relationship with other people. The M.C. is worldly achievement and position; the I.C. (Imum Coeli) is involvement with home and family, the base from which achievement launches.

Sign	Planet	House	Quality	Element
Aries	Mars	1st Angular	Cardinal	Fire
Taurus	Venus	2nd Succedent	Fixed	Earth
Gemini	Mercury	3rd Cadent	Mutable	Air
Cancer	Moon	4th Angular	Cardinal	Water
Leo	Sun	5th Succedent	Fixed	Fire
Virgo	Mercury	6th Cadent	Mutable	Earth
Libra	Venus	7th Angular	Cardinal	Air
Scorpio	Pluto: Mars	8th Succedent	Fixed	Water
Sagittarius	Jupiter	9th Cadent	Mutable	Fire
Capricorn	Saturn	10th Angular	Cardinal	Earth
Aquarius	Uranus: Saturn	11th Succedent	Fixed	Air
Pisces	Neptune: Jupiter	12th Cadent	Mutable	Water

Table of Correspondences

Planetary Strengths

When a planet is placed in its own sign it is said to be in dignity. There is a harmony between the principle of the planet and the expression of the sign; the planet is then able to operate strongly, in a direct and uncomplicated manner—but modified, of course, by other factors in the chart. A planet is in detriment when it is in the sign opposite to its dignity (Moon in Capricorn, Venus in Scorpio, etc.) and this placing tends to restrict the easy expression of the planetary energy.

There are certain other planetary sign placings which are known as exaltations. These signs seem not only to allow a planet to express strongly, but also to bring out an extra component of that planet, the possibility of a deeper creativitiy which may be a more

evolved expression of its potential. When it is in the opposite sign to
the exaltation, the planet is in its fall, an inhibiting condition which
can symbolically push that planet into the unconscious and distort
the beneficial manifestation of its energy.

Many modern astrolgers dismiss exaltation, detriments and falls
as antiquated concepts with no place in progressive astrological
theory. Certainly they should not be taken as direct interpretative
considerations, but they have survived in most textbooks with an
uncanny persistence. It is probable that they have a deeper
significance than is widely realized and that they lead us to a more
sensitive understanding of both the sign and the planet involved.
Appreciation of these inter-relationships will further help with the
art of synthesis.

A table of planetary strengths is given below. Alternative or
doubtful exaltations and falls are shown in brackets:

Planet	Sign Ruled	Detriment	Exaltation	Fall
Sun	Leo	Aquarius	Aries	Libra
Moon	Cancer	Capricorn	Taurus	Scorpio
Mercury	Gemini Virgo	Sagittarius Pisces	Virgo (Aquarius)	Pisces (Leo)
Venus	Taurus Libra	Scorpio Aries	Pisces	Virgo
Mars	Aries Scorpio	Libra Taurus	Capricorn	Cancer
Jupiter	Sagittarius Pisces	Gemini Virgo	Cancer	Capricorn
Saturn	Capricorn Aquarius	Cancer Leo	Libra	Aries
Uranus	Aquarius	Leo	Scorpio	Taurus
Neptune	Pisces	Virgo	(Cancer)	(Capricorn)
Pluto	Scorpio	Taurus	(Pisces) (Aquarius)	(Virgo) (Leo)

Table of Planetary Strengths

7.
PLANETS IN THE SIGNS AND HOUSES

The theme of this book is the movement from the relatively easy role of analysis to the more difficult, subtler art of synthesis. This section has more to do with analysis and although anyone approaching astrological interpretation for the first time will obviously need to refer to each of the paragraphs on the relevant planetary placings, it is important that the *quality* behind the placing is understood and that the interpretation alone is not merely learnt parrot-fashion. The latter approach leads to a string of part-related interpretation paragraphs—computers do this with speed and insensitivity.

The earlier chapter on the signs should be referred to for interpretation of the Sun or the Ascendant in each of the twelve signs. However, there are slight differences between these two expressions of each sign and these are considered below.

Always remember that the pure expression of the rising sign will be modified by any planet near the Ascendant or making close aspects to it and that the solar expression of any sign may be partly overshadowed by a strong group of planets (a stellium) in a different sign. Obey the rules of interpretation, work up from the keywords (if that feels right for you within your relationship with astrology) and try to be precise—but still always allow flexibility and flowingness in the interpretation. This will help synthesis.

Sun or Ascendant
Aries: Ascendant in Aries has a greater urgency than Sun in Aries. There is more restlessness and extroverted confidence, which sometimes appears to be an over-exaggeration. Sun in Aries has a little more maturity in the expression of the sign.

Taurus: The artistic quality of Taurus can express equally through Sun or Ascendant, but determination/stubbornness is often stronger when the sign is rising. Certainly the physical appearance is likely to be more thick-set. Sun in Taurus may gently emphasize the calm and possesive expressions of the sign.

Gemini: The witty chattiness of Gemini is usually stronger when the sign is rising and gesticulating hands are especially used to aid communication. The Sun brings out a 'quieter' (within Gemini's perpetual buzz) intellectual versatility.

Cancer: Pale skin, round face, loosely rounded mouth and an extra share of bodily fat are possible physical features more appropriate to Cancer rising than to Sun in Cancer. So also are the actively maternal qualities—protective caring and sometimes smothering. Sun in Cancer tends to express the sign's characteristics slightly more passively—the inherent active-passive conflict is not so obvious.

Leo: Ascendant Leo tends to emphasize the self-centering side of the sign—the pleasure of being on display, the expectation of recognition and the confidence of self importance. Sun Leo often does not need to apparently try so hard and can be somewhat more creative and benevolent. A flowing shock of hair and lion-like features correlate more with Ascendant than Sun.

Virgo: The appearance is neat and meticulous with Virgo on the Ascendant and the disposition is more earnest and a little more prone to worry than Sun Virgo, but the hard-working perfection-seeking qualities are applicable to both placings. Sun Virgo may show a little more confidence than Virgo rising.

Libra: The concern with social correctness, diplomacy and charm is stronger when Libra is rising—the sign of outward appearances at the most personally externalised part of the chart. When the Sun is in Libra, a different ascendant tones down these qualities of the sign and allows a more rounded expression.

Scorpio: This Ascendant seems to sharpen the conflict and tension inherent in Scorpio and create a stronger need to become involved with extremes of experience. Sun in Scorpio is often more easily able to express the positive characteristics of the sign. The deep, dark, penetrating gaze so typical of Scorpio is more noticeable when the sign is rising.

Sagittarius: Enthusiasm, wanderlust and heartiness are slightly more characteristic of the Sagittarian Ascendant than the Sun. Both placings have the need for independence, but the Sun can sometimes bring out a less irresponsible expression of the sign's qualities. A long jaw and long teeth are often seen with a Sagittarian Ascendant.

Capricorn: Angular and boney in appearance, Capricorn ascendant often results in delays in life—the goat's climb up the mountain does not bring its rewards until mature years. Sun Capricorn can lay more emphasis on achievement in the material world, on structure and responsibility, while there may be more potential for higher 'spiritual' achievement when the sign is rising.

Aquarius: There is perhaps less differentiation between Sun and Ascendant with Aquarius. Detached, inventive and humanitarian—the qualities of the sign apply equally. But there is sometimes less unease in close relationship when Aquarius is rising than with Sun in Aquarius and the problem of finding one's individuality is not so elusive.

Pisces: The caring, self-sacrificing qualities of Pisces and the ability to grasp intangibles apply for both Sun and Ascendant. But the sensitivity of the sign is felt much more on the Ascendant and often some sort of personality barrier is created as a survival mechanism. Pisces rising sometimes correlates with large, protruding eyes.

The house in which the Sun is placed will have its affairs emphasized in a central and important manner. This does not necessarily mean success or happiness connected with that house, but rather a focus of attention and experience to be applied. Additionally there will be a connection with the house which has Leo in its cusp. The meanings of the houses are given in a previous chapter.

Moon in Signs and Houses
Moon in Aries: The emotions and feelings are expressed strongly and powerfully. There is a 'no-nonsense' quality about this placing, which can give an appearance of insensitivity.

Moon in Taurus (Exaltation):   There is an uncomplicated responsiveness to natural sensual pleasures, a delight in the countryside and a strong emotional nature. The natural rhythms of life are appreciated and possessiveness is expressed gently and lovingly.

Moon in Gemini: The individual will be talkative, responding cheerfully to the ebb and flow of conversation. Moods may be diverse and changeable.

Moon in Cancer (Dignity):   Caring, responsive and instinctively nurturing, the individual enjoys emotional security and is able to give out a similar feeling to others.

Moon in Leo: Emotionally extravagent, the individual will need attention, appreciation and limelight. But generosity and warmth will be a natural response.

Moon in Virgo: The desire to be of service is strong, but emotions and feelings can be a little tight. This can result in an over-critical attitude to those with whom there is emotional contact.

Moon in Libra: The need for relationship is strong and emotional interaction with the partner is emphasized. The individual will be particularly responsive to beauty and harmony.

Moon in Scorpio (Fall):   The feelings are deep and intense. Emotional secrecy can cause an over-introspective nature. Jealousy can be a problem.

Moon in Sagittarius: An easy-going extraversion gives a warm emotional nature, but it is sometimes applied indiscriminantly and thoughtlessly.

Moon in Capricorn (Detriment):   At best emotional stability is given, but more commonly the placing results in inhibition, shyness and a difficulty in expressing feelings. This is often covered up by a serious attitude to material responsibility.

Moon in Aquarius: The individual is sensitive to wider, more humanitarian issues, but, although friendly, the placing nevertheless emphasizes coolness and emotional detachment.

Moon in Pisces: Extreme sensitivity is shown. Self-sacrificing love is freely given and the individual delights in being of service to those in need.

Moon in 1st: Sensitivity to other people and the environment is emphasized, sometimes resulting in touchiness. Swings of moods have to be reckoned with and there may be a close connection with the mother.

Moon in 2nd: Emotional life is important and financial or material security can become a strong need. This is aggravated by money matters and possessions being subject to changes.

Moon in 3rd: Conversation and the affairs of the immediate environment will play an important part in life. Education, reading and writing are enjoyed and there will be involvement with siblings or immediate family.

Moon in 4th: The home and the family will be a central concern. The security of these emotional ties will not only be needed but also appreciated and enjoyed.

Moon in 5th: The individual will be responsive to pleasure and recreation. Creativity will be appreciated, in others especially, although personal artistic expression is also possible. Children may play an important part in the emotional life.

Moon in 6th: Work of any sort is important and there is a need to be helpful to others. Concern about health, hygiene and diet is likely.

Moon in 7th: The individual will show especial sensitivity where close relationships are concerned. The emotional life with the partner is subject to fluctuation.

Moon in 8th: A deeper sensitivity to other people's emotions and affairs leads to intense feelings in such areas as sex, money and inner change.

Moon in 9th: Travel is enjoyed and there is a desire to become involved with deeper studies and philosophical thought.

Moon in 10th: The individual will need to feel involved in his career and his position in the wider environment, but ups and downs are likely. There is a need for recognition and involvement with the public is possible. There may be a close connection with the mother.

Moon in 11th: A responsiveness to friendship and to groups is indicated. There may be changeability in attitude to broader objectiveness in life.

Moon in 12th: Feelings are especially sensitive and have a hidden quality. The person will have periodic need for seclusion and inner nourishment.

Mercury in Signs and Houses

Mercury in Aries: The mind is sharp and incisive and there will be a direct, assertive way of communicating. Tactlessness is a possibility. Judgements and decisions are made quickly and intuitively.

Mercury in Taurus: Slow methodical thinking is likely, but a practical and thorough mental approach is also indicated. The singing voice is often good.

Mercury in Gemini (Dignity):   The intellect is versatile and clever, processing information quickly, often apparently dealing with a multiplicity of facts. Conversation can be witty and stimulating.

Mercury in Cancer: The mental approach is intuitive and the mind sensitive. Communication can be indirect, but the memory is usually good. Imagination is fertile, but sometimes sentimental.

Mercury in Leo (possible Fall):   The spoken word tends to be flamboyant, like an actor or orator, and communication in any form is expressed with confidence. Although creative expression is enhanced, personal opinions can be over-emphasized.

Mercury in Virgo (Dignity and Exaltation):   Mental ability is well organised and precise, but sometimes unadventurous. Studious by nature, the individual will communicate in an orderly manner, but often with too much concern for detail.

Mercury in Libra: Communication is pleasant and diplomatic and the intellect is active. There is a particular concern to achieve balanced judgements, but the individual will try to avoid unpleasant issues in discussion.

Mercury in Scorpio: Mental interests must probe beneath the surface and behind facades. This questioning nature needs to decipher and to understand the motivations behind human behaviour, but the individual is not necessarily open and forthcoming.

Mercury in Sagittarius (Detriment):   Enthusiasm for widely-ranging subjects can result in exaggeration and a lack of mental discipline. Broad principles are understood and philosophical subjects are appreciated, but this is often to the detriment of practicalities.

Mercury in Capricorn: The mental approach is efficient, practical and structured, giving an impression of cold efficiency in communication. But such a serious mentality lacks imagination and tends towards scepticism.

Mercury in Aquarius (possible Exaltation):   The mind is inventive and original and the individual is often intellectually brilliant, but the combination can lead to impractical eccentricities. There are no personal barriers to communication within what is seen as an idealistic brotherhood of man.

Mercury in Pisces (Detriment and Fall):   The mind is often confused and easily influenced in everyday matters. Understanding is possible on levels which the individual finds difficult to explain. Psychism is often highly developed, atmospheres are sensed and the dream life is rich.

N.B.   Mercury will always be placed in the same sign as the Sun or in one of the signs on either side. When in the same sign as the Sun there is perhaps a mental over-emphasis in terms of that sign. Mercury in a different sign often gives a more rounded intellect, being a balance of the two signs involved—but other factors in the chart must be considered.

Mercury in 1st: The person will have an intellectual and communicative approach to life. Mental activities are an important way of expressing his individuality.

Mercury in 2nd: Material rewards may come from mental work or communication of some nature. The individual may need to talk or write about feelings or material possessions and money.

Mercury in 3rd: The intellect will be active in all areas of communication—writing, reading, talking, teaching, learning. Mental interests will play an important part in a life which will be busy with activity and local travel.

Mercury in 4th: Mental interest will focus on home and family and there will be a strong need for communication within that environment. Thought may focus on considerations of security.

Mercury in 5th: Pleasure is gained from creative communication and writing and speaking skills are enhaced. Communication with children is good.

Mercury in 6th: The intellect is used in work or the work is connected with communication in some form. Busy mental activity is both practical and concerned with details.

Mercury in 7th: Communication in close personal relationship is an important factor and the individual needs to be aware of the opinions and thoughts of partners. Social discourse comes easily.

Mercury in 8th: The individual will be interested in deeper and more mysterious subjects—psychology, sex and the occult. Communication with others in close relationships will be intense and probing.

Mercury in 9th: More profound subjects like philosophy and religion will be of interest, but the intellectual approach may be impractical. Further education is likely to be important. Travel is also emphasised.

Mercury in 10th: Communication in some form will be associated with the career or outward expression in the world. Public speaking, lecturing, published writings, or involvement with the media are all possible.

Mercury in 11th: An emphasis in communication with friends and groups or societies will be likely. Wider social issues and life objectives occupy the mind and provide intellectual stimulus.

Mercury in 12th: Thoughts, intellectual interests and communications are kept private and introspective, partly because of difficulty in understanding clearly on a mental level. This is a good placing for involvement with psychic communication.

Venus in Signs and Houses

Venus in Aries (Detriment): The urge for relationship is expressed impulsively and forcefully. The individual may be predatory or lustful which can allow ardour and self-centredness to extinguish gentler harmonies and loving sensitivity.

Venus in Taurus (Dignity): Strong but harmonious sensuality expresses not only in relationships, but also artistically. Soft, natural colours and textures are enjoyed. Possessiveness in relationship stems from love and pleasure, not insecurity—the placing tends to bring stable partnerships and material benefits.

Venus in Gemini: Happy and communicative in the social whirl, the individual will nevertheless tend to be versatile or even changeable in personal relationships. A flirtatious nature can be entertaining and enjoyable, but superficiality is also a possibility, which could result in impermanence in relationships.

Venus in Cancer: Sentimental, emotionally caring relationships are indicated and there is a tendency to be clinging. Harmony is sought in the home and with the family and the individual expresses love gently and protectively, perhaps even maternally. Both sensitive treatment and romance are needed in relationships.

Venus in Leo: Generous and perhaps ostentatious in relationship, the individual is a loyal, warm and enthusiastic lover—but one who needs to be appreciated. Relationships and artistic activities are likely to be experienced as opportunities for self-expression.

Venus in Virgo (Fall): Discriminating as a lover, perhaps conservative or prudish in relationship, the individual may be too critical or restrained to be able to get full enjoyment from partnerships. Disappointment and dissatisfaction can result. This placing makes a better art critic than artist.

Venus in Libra (Dignity): Art, beauty, elegance, love and harmonious relationship are all indicated. Although a benign placing, there is a slightly idealized quality involved. The principle of artistic expression or the concept of the perfectly balanced relationship are more important than the reality of the art object or the marriage.

Venus in Scorpio (Detriment):   Relationships are experienced with intensity, as if they are being used for a purpose—inner growth, renewal or even material gain. Such deep passion, expressing with emotional complexity and powerful sexuality, can achieve heights and depths in relationship, often all or nothing.

Venus in Sagittatius: Enthusiastic and idealistic as a lover, the individual may nevertheless avoid deep involvement, which can be too restricting. A fun-loving, easy-going nature can turn into irresponsibility or amorality, but there is potential for expressing a more universal type of love. Often partners from foreign lands have an exotic attraction.

Venus in Capricorn: Relationship is taken seriously and although this does not inhibit involvement it may detract from enjoyment. Both love and art can be seen in terms of material value—the individual may marry for status or wealth and a thing of beauty will be a good investment for ever.

Venus in Aquarius: Both art and relationship are idealized, but love may be seen as just an extension of a very special friendship. The individual will be cool as a lover, but originality and a lack of convention can bring piquancy into a relationship. Social contacts are rich and diverse.

Venus in Pisces (Exaltation):   Loving, caring and unselfish, this placing gives sensitivity and compassion in relationship. The partner is everything, almost to the total denial of the self and sometimes this can lead to escapist indulgence in sensuality, but always love is there. Music and dance are often artistic interests.

Venus in 1st: Charming and extrovertedly attractive, the individual will have artistic tendencies and a sensual enjoyment of relationship. Active and assertive, the placing often allows a person to have what he wants.

Venus in 2nd: Financial and material matters are likely to be successful. Personal feelings of attraction will be strong, but the individual may be possessive in relationships.

Venus in 3rd: A charming and entertaining conversationalist, the person will be more of a social asset than an attentive partner. Active mental interest in the arts may be somewhat dilletante, but creative writing is often a talent.

Venus in 4th: Harmony and enjoyment in domestic matters is suggested and the home is likely to be comfortable and tastefully appointed. Relationship with the family is important. An inner balance and harmony leads to feelings of security and the later years of life are likely to be pleasant.

Venus in 5th: Creative talents, recreation and romance are all enjoyed. The individual may also have a sensually dramatic nature and personal charisma. Children can bring happiness.

Venus in 6th: Work is a pleasure and the person will want working conditions to be harmonious. Relationship with working colleagues and employees should be good. Work in the arts is a possibility.

Venus in 7th: Close personal relationships are important and the partner may be artistic, beautiful or a financial asset. The social life is likely to be active. Satisfaction and enjoyment are derived from sharing as many activities as possible with the partner.

Venus in 8th: The emotional and sexual expressions of relationships are a preoccupation, potentially able to transform the people involved. Business instinct is likely to be good and financial benefit can come from partners and legacies.

Venus in 9th: Travel brings enjoyment and benefit. There is also a desire to bring people together, through deeper understanding of each other and through knowledge of philosophies and religion.

Venus in 10th: Career and social position are likely to be successful and the individual may be publicly popular. Artistic professions are indicated, but fashion, entertainment, beauty and diplomacy are also possibilities.

Venus in 11th: Much pleasure is derived from friends and associates. Groups and gatherings connected with the arts and culture are enjoyed and there is an interest in social issues and values.

Venus in 12th: Relationship is treated personally and privately—clandestine affairs are also possible. But compassion and unselfishness are indicated, with the result that love may be expressed in service to others.

Mars in Signs and Houses

Mars in Aries (Dignity):   Drive and ambition are vigorous and direct. Although brave and adventurous, the individual can be insensitive to other people. Sexuality is strong, but the individual may not cater for the partner's needs.

Mars in Taurus (Detriment):   Material gain is important and effort for this will be applied persistently. A strong sexual expression is sensual and earthly, but sometimes over possessive. A deep temper may be prone to sudden explosion.

Mars in Gemini: Energy is applied enthusiastically in many different areas, usually connected with the intellect and communication, but it is often spread too thinly. A rapier wit and versatile sexuality both need varying stimuli.

Mars in Cancer (Fall):   The individual finds it difficult to be direct and tries to achieve his aims obliquely or manipulatively. Indecisiveness or fussiness may result. A latent insecurity may result in sexual underconfidence or laziness.

Mars in Leo: Confidence in action and great personal magnetism are indicated. Energy is expressed flamboyantly and the individual will know what he wants and expect to get it. He will expect to be appreciated in all matters, including lovemaking.

Mars in Virgo: The person will be more of an enthusiastic worker than an ardent lover. Energy is expressed analytically and precisely—this may be efficient, but it can restrict initiative.

Mars in Libra (Detriment):   Although this is a non-aggressive, indecisive placing, arguments are possible, particularly with partners. Moderation is always likely, but skill in strategic matters is often indicated.

Mars in Scorpio (Dignity):   The desire for power is strong and the fight will be intense, but often behind the scenes. Sexual expression is seen as an important way of deepening emotional involvement with another person and intense passion is usually present.

Mars in Sagittarius: Energy and action tend to be enthusiastic, but over-ambitious. The person desires adventure, but has a reluctance to accept responsibility—independence is in the blood and new horizons always beckon. His zeal can often become militant fanaticism.

Mars in Capricorn (Exaltation):   The individual is ambitious and will express energy with constructive efficiency, so that the top rung of the ladder will be reached and the rewards achieved. Sexual expression may be restrained, but a power-seeking urge is not far beneath the surface.

Mars in Aquarius: There is a dynamic, unconventional power in this placing, but its highly-charged nature can result in erratic behaviour. The individual may fight for causes or social issues or inspire others to do so, or he may need to express his inventiveness in some more individualized manner—progressive or eccentric.

Mars in Pisces: Action and energy are diffused and diluted in this placing, resulting in confusion, misdirection and inconsistency. Sometimes the intangible forces can be harnessed in unpublicised selfless service. Sexuality may be over-influenced by an emotional sensuality.

Mars in 1st: Fearless and impulsive, the individual desires to prove himself and dominate the environment. He is likely to be tough in body and determined in character.

Mars in 2nd: Much attention and energy is given to achieving material gain, but often the application is so avid that it is counterproductive. Rashness and extravagence can be financially destructive.

Mars in 3rd: Assertive in all aspects of communication, this placing can sometimes lead to quarrelsome discussion. The mind is often over-active or highly-strung.

Mars in 4th: There is a focus of activity in the home and with the family. Often the individual will try and dominate in these areas, resulting in friction and emotional turbulence.

Mars in 5th: Individuality is powerfully expressed in creative pursuits, romantic liaisons and recreation. Egotism may dominate, causing problems with speculation or friction with lovers or children.

Mars in 6th: Much effort is applied in work, but the individual can become a hard task-master—his own natural industrious energy is perhaps unreasonably expected of colleagues and employees.

Mars in 7th: This placing is sexually assertive in relationships, but can also bring friction and strife into both love relationships and business partnerships. Energy can express as domination or, more usefuly, as cooperation.

Mars in 8th: There is a desire for deep involvement with the partner. This can express through a strong sex drive, a sharing of inner emotions or a financial partnership, but the result tends to be extreme—either transformation or destruction.

Mars in 9th: The individual is likely to travel enthusiastically or partake in sports—there is a restless need for adventure. Opinions are held strongly, often with religious fervour.

Mars in 10th: Ambition is strong and energy is applied assertively in the chosen career or profession. The individual can be aggressively competitive within the career structure.

Mars in 11th: Keeness and active enthusiasm are shown for causes, objectives and ideals. Friendships are pursued with energy, but excessive drive can cause friction, both with friends and in involvement with groups.

Mars in 12th: Much activity occurs behind the scenes, often for the good of others, but this can also lead to conflict with hidden enemies. Desires or sexuality may be repressed or confused.

Jupiter in Signs and Houses

Jupiter in Aries: Positive, optimistic and enthusiastic, the individual has big ideas for projecting himself into the world. This can either create personal opportunities and growth or over-inflation. Travel is energetically enjoyed.

Jupiter in Taurus: Successful and generous with money and material possessions, the individual may have a sensually indulgent streak which can result in self-aggrandisement or expansion of the waistline. However there is potential to bring ideals and philosophies into practical reality.

Jupiter in Gemini (Detriment):   Much enjoyment is experienced in mental activity and conversation, but the placing encourages verbosity and superficiality. Broad principles and deeper philosophies are unsuitable for Gemini's quick, slick computer circuitry. But potentially the placing can bring conciseness to abstract ideas.

Jupiter in Cancer (Exaltation):   Compassionate and generous, the individual enjoys all matters connected with family and home. Emotional responsiveness and a feeling of protectiveness can bring a sense of personal reward and there is usually a pleasant security felt in religious faith.

Jupiter in Leo: Although jovial and benevolent, the placing can inflate the ego and bring excessive pride. This sense of self-importance can make the person pompous, but for all this he may still be engaging and likeable, possessing a certain ability to pass on the wisdom of experience.

Jupiter in Virgo (Detriment):   Enjoyment and opportunity are restricted by the need to scrutinize and criticize anything outside immediately categorized spheres of experience. Religious beliefs are likely to be conservative—or non-existent because of scepticism.

Jupiter in Libra: Wisdom, and often happiness, is gained through the experience of relationship and social intercourse, but the individual may never want to be alone. Companionship in travel and more serious studies brings enjoyment.

Jupiter in Scorpio: There is an intense and serious need to understand the deeper mysteries of life and to penetrate behind surface teachings and dogma. Desire for power, wealth and control of others is sometimes increased.

Jupiter in Sagittarius (Dignity): Extrovert and warmly enthusiastic, the individual needs to explore all aspects of life—broadening the mind through travel and study. But the surpreme expansiveness of the placing may result in exaggeration and restless behaviour, spreading the energy too widely to achieve focus.

Jupiter in Capricorn (Fall): Often successful in career and material achievement, the individual nevertheless feels an inner conflict between the need for visible success or largesse and the conservation of his personal riches and his executive influence.

Jupiter in Aquarius: The individual is able to take a broad view of social and humanitarian issues. This makes him something of an idealist, but he derives enjoyment from making his contribution through impersonal contact with others. He can impart progressive knowledge by his personal example.

Jupiter in Pisces (Dignity): Faith, sincerity and kindliness stem from this placing. Happiness and peace are found in spiritual rather than material wealth. But such extensive openess often results in poor judgement and inability to discriminate.

Jupiter in 1st: Optimistic, extrovert and cheerful, this popular individual will attract good fortune and inspire confidence in others. Opportunites can be grasped; travel, adventure and higher studies are enjoyed. A tendency to over-reach must be avoided.

Jupiter in 2nd: Financial success and material good fortune are likely and the individual is in tune with the earth's resources. Overspending and taking gambles are both possibilities.

Jupiter in 3rd: Enjoyment and possible success are derived from reading, writing and learning. Wide mental development is possible. Happiness and benefit may come from close relatives and neighbours.

Jupiter in 4th: A happy home and family life is suggested. Benefits may come from the parents or perhaps later in life. Often a sense of inner security and well-being is experienced.

Jupiter in 5th: Self-expression through creative activities, sport, recreation, romance and speculation may bring happiness and enjoyment—often 'good luck' as well. Pleasure, and sometimes benefit, come from children.

Jupiter in 6th: Work is enjoyed and relations with employees and colleagues are likely to be harmonious. Success and reward may come from service to other people.

Jupiter in 7th: Relationships, marriage and business partnership are likely to be happy and enjoyable, with the possibility of material benefit from them. A helpful and co-operative attitude contributes to social and financial success.

Jupiter in 8th: The individual will tend to see the best in other people, often receiving financial benefits from them. Enjoyment and satisfaction are found in deeper personal relationships and sexual expression. Mystical and occult matters may provide special interest.

Jupiter in 9th: Optimistic in outlook, the individual will derive enjoyment and success from higher education, philosophy and religion. Prophecy and good judgement are possible, if a tendency towards exaggeration is curtailed. Much travel is indicated.

Jupiter in 10th: Success and enjoyment in the chosen career are indicated. Wide influence and accomplishment are likely, resulting in professional recognition.

Jupiter in 11th: Many friendships are enjoyed and the individual has the ability to bring groups of people together for the common good. Benefits are likely from friends and groups and the realization of hopes and personal objectives should be possible.

Jupiter in 12th: The individual is philanthropic and compassionate. Enjoyment and inner rewards are derived from helping other people in unostentatious, self-sacrificing ways. Benefits, unsought, tend to arrive when they are needed, but unrealistic generosity may be a problem.

Saturn in Signs and Houses

Saturn in Aries (Fall):   The individual has difficulty with self-assertion and is likely to be lacking in self-confidence. Either he will be reluctant to push himself forward or he will try and impose a harsh discipline on others. The lesson is to learn the harmonious expression of both self-discipline and self-assertiveness.

Saturn in Taurus: The relationship with money, possessions and natural resources is awkward. Insecurity may lead to a grasping possessiveness and emotional stinginess. The individual lacks freedom to enjoy simple sensual pleasures and austerity may result. The lesson is to learn to trust the natural expressions of beauty and emotions and to allow material rewards to come in their own time.

Saturn in Gemini: There may be severe doubts about personal intellectual ability and versatility. This either results in a slow-witted, depressive quality or an exaggerated need to work hard at studies and mental improvement. The individual needs to transform this underconfidence into a mental discipline which will bring depth to Gemini's superficiality.

Saturn in Cancer (Detriment):   Worries about the family and fears of losing emotional security restricts the easy flow of caring feelings and the crab's shell may become a fixed barrier. The individual either becomes seriously over-protective or doubts his ability to make a contribution as a parent and shuts off his emotions. The lesson involves developing emotional expression and learning to trust that security is only an attitude of mind—it exists within the individual and not in the outer world.

Saturn in Leo (Detriment):   Happy and creative self-expression is difficult to achieve. Leo's normally centred self-confidence is undermined and this usually results in over-compensating autocratic behaviour. The individual needs to learn to accept warmth from others and to allow himself to reflect it back. He also needs to make a realistic evaluation of his own potential and build a balanced self-confidence.

Saturn in Virgo: This placing can over-emphasize a desire for order and detail, creating anxiety when such precision is absent. The individual may be preoccupied with personal shortcomings and may obsessively need to apply extra exertion in order to compensate. Moderation needs to be learned and discrimination developed, whilst trusting that the work in hand will be achieved efficiently and effectively.

Saturn in Libra (Exaltation):   Concern with relationship, harmony and partnership is expressed seriously and in a disciplined manner. Behind this there is often doubt and fear, which can result in rejection of partnership or artisitic activities. Alternatively, exaggerated seriousness makes heavy weather of relationship. But the opportunity is for balance and correctness in all social pairings—fidelity, integrity and decorum.

Saturn in Scorpio: There is likely to be resistance to allowing the open expression of passion, sexuality and strong feelings. Power and control become an issue, both desired and feared, and consequently repression can result. Over-compensation shows as cold and ruthless power-seeking and perhaps emotional and sexual control. The individual needs to learn to express his inner feelings as they really are, without guilt or fear, secretly if necessary. He can then enable inner transformation to take place.

Saturn in Sagittarius: Freedom of thought and action are restricted by a mistrust of overenthusiasm and of too much independence. Faith and religious belief do not come easily and yet the individual yearns to be able to cut loose the bonds and to soar. The placing enables him to learn to bring abstract concepts into practical reality and to stabilize the conflict between his rigid dogmatism and his quest for truth.

Saturn in Capricorn (Dignity):   There is a serious attitude to material achievement and a strong need for organization and structure. Fear of failure or disintegration can result in selfishness and a cold disregard for others. The balanced expression of this placing brings endurance, patience and a skill for long-range planning. The individual must develop a knowledge that he can reach his goals surely and smoothly, without anxiety or deprivation.

Saturn in Aquarius (Dignity):   A mistrust of new and progressive ideas can lead to an obstinate attitude and a desire to impose discipline and structure on others. There may be a fear of becoming over involved with idealistic ventures and initiative can be restricted. The person needs to cultivate a more humanitarian approach and to accept the value of originality and inventiveness. This will allow Aquarian ideals and progressive ideas to be grounded and brought into practical manifestation.

Saturn in Pisces: Self-discipline and self-reliance do not come easily to the individual, often resulting in muddled indecisiveness and feeling of guilt. Compassionate feelings are difficult to express and there is a fear of letting go. The lessons to be learned involve acceptance, caring, self-sacrifice and renunciation—one must allow the self to flow with the cosmic stream.

Saturn in 1st: Expression of individual initiative and self assertiveness do not come easily, often resulting in self-repression or excessive self-discipline. Compensation for this may be sought in hardness, domination of others and an unbending attitude. The lesson is to learn a balanced self-confidence, so that the individual can put himself forward where appropriate, without relying on aggressive behaviour.

Saturn in 2nd: The placing brings anxiety about material insecurity. This concern creates the need to work harder than necessary to earn money and such a negative attitude can also lead to financial difficulties. Sometimes worry about possessions leads to miserliness. The individual needs to learn the proper and balanced handling of personal resources.

Saturn in 3rd: Often early education is hard or perhaps curtailed. There is a feeling of inadequacy in writing, talking, reading and studying so that an extra effort has to be made in these areas to compensate. The lesson is one of intellectual self-discipline, learning to organise facts and apply commonsense and concentration in any area of communication.

Saturn in 4th: An inner feeling of insecurity leads to fear of losing the home or base in life. Domestic responsibilities are taken seriously. Sometimes there may be an abreaction and family life is shunned—this is a misplaced protection against losing that security. The individual must learn to develop a balanced attitude of responsibility to the family and to realise that lessons can be learned from the experience of the relationships with parents and other family members.

Saturn in 5th: The individual finds it difficult to have fun in life and feels uncomfortable about relaxing and enjoying life's pleasures—he may also be afraid of allowing himself mild personal indulgencies. This restricts both creative output and romance and it can cause difficulty with children or speculative ventures. He needs to confront these attitudes and learn to develop his personal creative self-expression in whatever ways are appropriate. However pleasures are likely to be taken seriously.

Saturn in 6th: Underconfidence in working ability can lead to under-achievement or the feeling that it is necessary to do 120 per cent in order to achieve 100 per cent; this often creates a workaholic. The individual must learn to stabilize his working attitude, allowing his sense of duty and service to express with conscientiousness and responsibility, but without overcompensation and anxiety.

Saturn in 7th: Relationships and business partnerships may be frustrated; marriage can occur later in life and the partner may be older. Certainly any relationship is approached with caution due to mistrust, fear or underconfidence. Lessons have to be learned through the experience of close relationships with others and the responsibilities which follow from them.

Saturn in 8th: Heavy responsibilities may come from other people's financial affairs and there may be a reluctance to become deeply involved in any way with others. There is often sexual underconfidence, resulting in repression or distortion; a fear of death and of the occult is also possible. Lessons are learned through the experience of deeper emotional relationships and involvement with other people's resources. Confrontation of sexual issues may be necessary.

Saturn in 9th: Travel is usually not enjoyed and higher study or further education may either be felt lacking or be avoided because of feelings of inadequacy. Sometimes a strict religious upbringing has destroyed faith or produced strict fanatical attitudes. The individual must learn to stabilize and control in these areas, bringing balance to philosophical attitudes and religious beliefs. Negative attitudes to travel and further education may need confronting and resolving.

Saturn in 10th: There is usually a relentless urge for achievement, often compensating for a fear of failure in the world or the need to satisfy parental expectations. The individual has to strive hard and perhaps suffer delays and difficulty in the world, but he can realize his destiny successfully if these factors are confronted and transformed into self-reliance and independent achievement.

Saturn in 11th: The individual experiences difficulty or feels uncomfortable with friends and groups, resulting in over-discriminating attitudes or excessive seriousness in such circumstances. But lessons can be learned from these involvements and friendships can be valuable and enduring.

Saturn in 12th: It is possible that inner sorrow will be experienced and secretly endured. A fear of loneliness or rejection makes it difficult or even impossible for the person to provide spiritual nourishment for himself. Dark doubts and hidden anxieties may develop, which can breed insecurity and underconfidence. These negative emotions need to be confronted and lessons are learned through seclusion, service and inner experience.

The Outer Planets
Uranus, Neptune and Pluto spend so many years in each sign that their influence by sign applies more to generations and to large groups of people and is less relevant to individuals (but note the comments on page 27). Accordingly only the house placings of these outer planets are included here.

Uranus in the Houses
Uranus in 1st: Original and individualistic, perhaps even eccentric, the person is likely to be restless, highly-strung and unpredictable. His life will be affected by sudden changes and he may be involved with science, electronics and new inventions.

Uranus in 2nd: The attitude to material possessions is unconventional and finances are subject to erratic and extreme fluctuations.

Uranus in 3rd: The mentality is highly original and inventive. Conversation and communication may be abrupt and unpredictble. The attitude to education is non-conformist and there may have been changes in schooling.

Uranus in 4th: Many changes of residence are suggested, often sudden. Home and family circumstances are unusual and there may be friction where social traditions are concerned.

Uranus in 5th: Creative expression is ingenious and experimental; love affairs may be bizarre and subject to changes. Any children will be individualistic and unconventional and there may be turbulent relationships with them.

Uranus in 6th: Unless inventive or unusual work is found, there are likely to be many changes. Working skills will be unique and innovative.

Uranus in 7th: The probability of sudden breaks in close personal relationships, often divorce, can be avoided by establishing unconventional or even bizarre partnerships.

Uranus in 8th: There may be unusual or even eccentric interest in the occult and the deeper mysteries. Emotional relationships with others will be erratic and unpredictable and sexual desires may be unconventional. Unexpected financial benefits are possible.

Uranus in 9th: Attitudes to philosophy and religion are non-conformist and inconoclastic. Sudden unexpected travel is possible.

Uranus in 10th: Sudden changes or unexpected advancement in career are possible. An unusual job or progressive career environment is preferred—surroundings where inventiveness can flourish.

Uranus in 11th: Independent-minded or bohemian friends and associates are attracted and their company enjoyed. Personal objectives and ideals are forward-looking and out of the ordinary.

Uranus in 12th: The individual may have a strange and turbulent inner life or unusual psychic experiences, but he is likely to keep them to himself, possibly due to uncertainty about their meaning.

Neptune in the Houses

Neptune in 1st: The individual is sensitive, impressionable and imaginative, but also confused about his identity and he may be prone to self-deception. His intuition will be strong and he may even be psychic, but he must be beware of losing his head in the clouds.

Neptune in 2nd: There is an other-worldly attitude to material possessions. money is usually available, but the financial situation is confused and loss through fraud or deception is possible.

Neptune in 3rd: The mind is highly intuitive and imaginative, but easily muddled in everyday matters. Communication through art, music and poetry is indicated.

Neptune in 4th: The domestic scene may be somewhat over-idealized and self-sacrifice may be required. Confusion over emotional security or a feeling of inner uncertainty is likely, but inspiration and refinement may be developed within the family environment.

Neptune in 5th: There is a dramatized love of pleasure in this placing. Show-business interests and artistic creativity are indicated and love affairs may be chaotic or self-sacrificing. Recreation has escapist tendencies.

Neptune in 6th: Working abilities are more imaginative and altruistic than practical. It is difficult for the person to concentrate on his work and the job environment may be confused.

Neptune in 7th: The individual may have an over-idealized view of close relationships and be easily influenced by his partner. A higher, spiritual love may be sought, but ephemeral satisfaction or delusion is often only what is found.

Neptune in 8th: Sensitivity to occult and mystical matters is indicated, but dealings with financial and material resources may be subject to deceptive difficulties. Fantasy and disillusion can affect sexuality.

Neptune in 9th: A religious or spiritualistic attitude to life is likely. This can be either a source of deep inspiration or an influence bringing superstition and delusion.

Neptune in 10th: The individual will have idealized aspirations in the world which can lead to career fluctuation and confusion. Careers in films and glamorous professions are possible, but the public imge may be susceptible to scandal.

Neptune in 11th: Friends will be sensitive, artistic and perhaps spiritually inclined, but they may also be unreliable and manipulative. The individual is likely to have humanitarian ideals, but he should guard against unrealistic objectives in life.

Neptune in 12th: Extreme sensitivity can be usefully channelled into a life of service and sacrifice, but there may be an over-active imagination which can lead to irrational fears, often about seclusion.

Pluto in the Houses

Pluto in 1st: A powerful personality with a great sense of self-sufficiency is indicated. Life will be marked by continuous transformations, a series of endings and beginnings, and the individual will be something of a loner. A desire to control others may express through money and sexuality.

Pluto in 2nd: The attitude to money and possessions may tend to be obsessive and gains may be realized in mining or research. But the pathway between dramatic financial success and annihilation is a narrow one and both extremes may occur.

Pluto in 3rd: The mind needs to probe and penetrate. Ideas and opinions are subject to changes and renewal as new information is uncovered, but the intensity of the placing may lead to mental instability.

Pluto in 4th: The domestic environment may be explosive or lead to circumstances of great transformation. The family may be particularly important psychologically and there is deep inner need to investigate the effects of one's traditions and roots.

Pluto in 5th: Desire for creative expression is vital and unrestrained and personal growth may be connected with children. Romance and love affairs are handled inpetuously and with passion.

Pluto in 6th: This placing brings power and intensity to any work which is done. Often there is skill in research or the ability to transform and vitalize the working environment by the introduction of new methods.

Pluto in 7th: There are powerful and explosive forces associated with close personal relationships, but often they remain partly hidden. Involvements may be compulsive, but there is usually a vital opportunity for personal growth through the partner.

Pluto in 8th: An urge for power and a deep need for transformation is intense. It can operate as financial upheaval or through emotional turbulence and power games in relationships, but it does give the individual great fortitude and strength in the darker more difficult encounters in life.

Pluto in 9th: Inner growth and perhaps peak experiences can be achieved through involvement with philosophy, metaphysics and deeper studies. Travel may also open the doors of perception, but mind expanison through drugs and other 'short cuts' may be particularly dangerous.

Pluto in 10th: This placing indicates a powerful and influential position in society, but one which is likely to be operating out of the public eye. Not only is inner personal growth possible through the career, but there is also the ability to galvanize a business or an organisation into a new and vital state.

Pluto in 11th: Friendships are intense, not especially numerous and are subject to periodic upheavals. Connections with groups may have an important influence on personal development or there may be involvement with idealistic pressure groups or political reformers.

Pluto in 12th: The life is characterized by a relentless inner turbulence which may be only partly understood. This can provide a beneficial cleansing force within, although at times it may appear more destructive than helpful.

8.
THE ASPECTS

Approach to Interpretation

The aspects in astrology are the angular relationships between planets in the birth chart. They bring the concept of number symbolism directly into chart interpretation and they represent a dynamic energy pattern which can link the chart together. Planets which are very close together in zodiacal longitude in the birth chart or which are opposite or 90° apart or at other critical distances from each other, plus or minus a certain allowable factor, are said to be 'in aspect'. This means that the energies of the planets involved are fused together and the combination is made available to the individual for use in character expression and life development.

Traditional astrology books are categoric in stating that there are 'good' and 'bad' aspects. A good aspect, the traditionalists believe, will always bring good fortune and happiness, while the bad aspects are said to produce nothing but difficulties, hardship and misery—the implication is that plague, pestilence and famine is the only possible outcome. Fortunately, the interpretation of the aspects need in no way be rigid. Such an attitude represents an unhealthy, fatalistic view of astrology and implies that each individual is bound by the chains of his chart. But the exhortation over the entrance to the temple in ancient Delphi, 'Know Thyself', points towards the key with which we can unlock the chains. Personal psychological development, self-examination and consciousness allow us to use the energies in the chart positively and to rise above restrictions and difficulties—such as those which are implied by the so-called 'bad' aspects.

With the evolution of astrological understanding, the incorporation of psycholgical knowledge and the recognition of the need for personal responsibility, the modern approach to aspect interpretation is that there are no totally 'good' or totally 'bad' aspects. Any aspect is the combination of the energies of the two planets involved and that combination can be used constructively or negatively. Some energy combinations flow more harmoniously within the individual and are easier to apply advantageously in the world, while others will require more work and effort to find the positive expression. The less harmonious aspects (or an easier aspect between two planets which are incompatible, like Mars and Saturn) have a line of least resistance which can lead towards difficulty, problems and non-constructive results. If it is left to its own devices and if the individual turns a blind eye to that side of his character and tries to sweep it under the carpet (what the psychologist would call repression) then the effect of the aspect is not beneficial. These are the circumstances where the traditionalists would make their prognostication about 'malefic influences'.

But if the traditionalists had opened their awareness a little and taken the process one step further they would have realized that with personal work and self-examination any aspect energy can be transformed into a positive strength. Such work is not always simple and the effort may have to be sustained for many years or re-applied at various important periods in the life, but always there is a positive potential in what may seem to be the toughest of aspect patterns. It is relevant here to reiterate the reincarnation attitude to astrology. If the soul chooses the birth chart, then it also chooses any difficult aspect patterns and it follows that there must be a reason for this. In its wisdom, the soul wanted to experience a life symbolized by a chart with such aspect patterns and to learn to grow and evolve through that experience. It is possible that little advantage in terms of soul evolution would accrue if those aspects were ignored and unconsciously allowed to influence life and character in various disadvantageous and non-constructive ways.

The so-called difficult aspects also act as challenge and incentive. In a chart where all the aspects are harmonious, the individual will be tempted to let life flow smoothly by. There is nothing in the chart to stimulate activity. By and large life is pleasantly agreeable and the talents and gifts represented by the aspects may not become fully realized. The parable of the talents in the bible is worth pondering on with reference to astrological interpretation. Talents which are not invested at a good interest and which remain buried underground are not only wasted, but often also contribute to 'weeping and wailing and gnashing of teeth'.

In a chart where the aspects are not so easy the individual must confront the issues involved. If he does not, then life will throw confrontations at him with a vengeance and, if he still tries to turn a blind eye, a vicious downwards spiral of difficulty can result. Uncomfortable aspects in a chart provide the goad and the challenge to stimulate the individual to achievement—not necessarily worldly success, but achievement as measured on a personal, inner reference.

So even the most apparently difficult aspect can bring advantage and the most apparently benevolent aspect can leak away and become diluted in a listless ocean.

Conjunction

The easiest aspect to understand, and to find, is the conjunction. Two planets which are on the same degree of the zodiac or anything up to eight degrees apart are conjunct. This aspect has the numerological symbolism of unity, the single point, both zero and infinity, and represents a direct and simple fusion of the planetary energies involved.

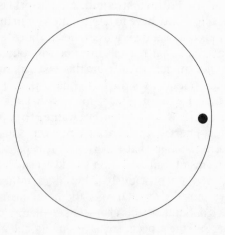

Figure 13.

The degree of ease or difficulty will depend on the nature of the planets involved. Usually the two planets will be in the same sign. The symbol for the conjunction is ☌ .

Many astrologers find that drawing lines between planets in aspect creates a visual pattern which aids interpretation and synthesis. (See chart example on page 62.)

Opposition

Two planets 180° apart are in opposition. This aspect divides the zodiac circle into two and implies duality—positive-negative, masculine-feminine, yin-yang.

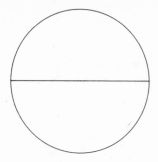

Figure 14.

Although the combined planetary energy will be subject to conflict and tension, the potential in this aspect is nevertheless one of balance. If we can hold the tension of opposites within us, accepting that paradoxes can exist, then a third resultant force may develop, contributing towards creative growth. The two planets involved will normally both be in signs of the same quality, both either positive or negative. The orb allowed is 8° and the symbol for the opposition is ☍.

Trine

Planets 120° apart are in trine aspect to each other. This is the three-fold division of the zodiac and represents a dynamic trinity of harmonious energy.

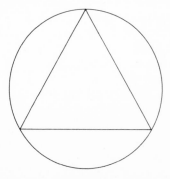

Figure 15.

The combination of the two planets can be used advantageously and with a relaxed ease, but the aspect is not as strong as is often implied and it requires some effort to bring out the full potential suggested by the fusion of the two planets. They will usually both be in signs of the same element. The orb allowed is 8° and the symbol for the trine is △.

Square

Planets 90° apart are in square aspect to each other. This represents a division of the zodiac circle into four and can be viewed as a strong cruciform structure upon which many of life's tests are fixed within the individual's character.

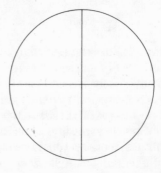

Figure 16.

It is an aspect which cannot be evaded, for it acts like a sharp and jangling spur to the horse travelling on the high road. Usually the two planets in square aspect will be in signs of the same quality but different polarities and therefore conflicting elements—fire and water, earth and air; water and air, earth and fire. This symbolizes the frustration experienced in the square aspect, but also points to the essential lessons to be learned so that the constructive effects of the planetary combination can be realized. The orb allowed is 8° and the symbol is □.

Sextile

Planets separated by 60° are in sextile aspects. The sixfold division has the quality of the hexagram or the six-pointed star. The latter is formed by two equilateral triangles, one pointing upwards like man reaching for the heavens and the other pointing downwards like spirit searching for manifestation in the physical world. The two triangles are harmoniously integrated.

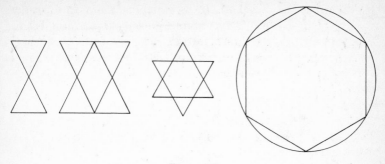

Figure 17.

The sextile is a more benevolent aspect than the trine and provides opportunity for the most constructive working out of the combined planetary energies involved. The planets are normally in signs of the same polarity and different, but harmonious elements. The orb allowed varies, but 5° is preferred. The symbol is **∗**.

Semi-Square and Sesqui-Quadrate

If the cross of the square aspect is further divided into eight, two minor inharmonious aspects are revealed.

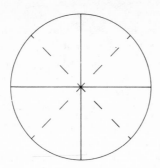

Figure 18.

Two planets 45° apart ('half a square') are in semi-square aspect; if 135° apart ('a square and a half') then they are in sesqui-quadrate aspect. Both tend towards a frustrated energy expression and conscious work is needed to overcome this and use the aspects constructively. The orb allowed is 2° and the symbols are ∠ & ⌑ respectively.

Quincunx

Two planets 150° apart are said to be in quincunx aspect, often also known as inconjunct. Often underestimated, this aspect brings further tests and lessons to be learned in the life and character. Its strain and conflict can be seen in the fact that the two planets will usually be in signs of conflicting polarity, element and quality. The orb allowed is 2° and the symbol is ⊼.

Minor Harmonious Aspects

Semi-sextile: A very gentle influence, the two planets being 30° apart, ±2°. The symbol is ⊻.
Quintile: The division of the zodiac into five, the number of Man—the planets are 72° apart, ±2°. The influence is especially harmonious, but delicate and subtle, so great sensitivity is needed to draw out the potential and talent offered. The symbol is Q.
Septile: Dividing the zodiac by the mystically symbolic number seven produces a separation of 51¾° (±2°) between planets in septile aspect. The symbol is S. The influence is even more subtle than the quintile and neither aspect need have regular application in the normal run of chart interpretation.

Further Considerations

1. *Orbs:*   There are no hard and fast rules regarding orbs. Two planets in exact aspect always have an intensity and compulsiveness in their effect, but it is not possible to say at what degree distance the effect stops. It is like asking at what moment does the sound of a gong die away—it depends upon the strength of the beat, the sensitivity of the ear, the amount of background noise and the acoustics of the environment. It is advisable for each individual to decide on orbs with which he or she feels comfortable after reading various authors' opinions—but to allow flexibility. For example: Sun and Jupiter are in square, but Jupiter and Venus are just out of orb for the square. If Sun and Venus are conjunct, perhaps it may be relevant, in that particular chart, to allow a square between Venus and Jupiter.

Some astrologers allow orbs of 10° or even 12° for aspects involving the Sun, Moon or ruling planets and orbs for sextiles range from 4° to 6°. It is as well to remember that the tighter the orbs used, the less aspects there will be to consider—but they will perhaps be the most important ones. When wide orbs are preferred, more aspects must be considered; but in certain cases it could be possible for the same two planets to be joined by two aspects of

differing influence. The ridiculous extreme is that everything ends
up by being aspect to almost everything else, making interpretation
impossible.

2. *Mutual Reception:*   Where two planets are in the signs ruled
by each other (e.g. Moon in Aries, Mars in Cancer) they are said to
be in mutual reception. This relationship can be treated like a
minor contact, either harmonious or inharmonious, but if the
planets are also in aspect (e.g. Moon square Mars), the latter takes
preference.

3. *Dissociate Aspects:*   The signs in which the aspecting planets
are placed usually have either a harmonious or inharmonious
relationship, depending on the aspect—for example planets in trine
are usually in signs of the same element. But, because of orbs used,
aspects can sometimes be in signs which do not have this expected
relationship and in this event they are known as dissociate aspects.
The simplest example is to consider a conjunction between Venus
in 29½° Aries and Mars in ½° Taurus. These planets are closely
conjunct, but dissociate. This phenomena detracts from the simple
expression of that aspect, but the interpretative relevance will
almost certainly be covered by consideration of the planets in their
signs. This aspect is also a mutual reception and it is a useful
exercise to ponder on the difference in interpretation and effect if
this sensually powerful conjunction was either completely in Aries,
in Taurus or dissociate as given in the example.

4. *Applying and Separating:*   The planets move at different
speeds and therefore, with the elapse of time, any aspect would
become more exact (applying) or wider (separating). Moon at 10°
Aries square Saturn at 15° Cancer is applying. Venus at 25°
Gemini opposition Neptune at 20° Sagittarius is separating. Where
other factors are equal, an applying aspect is stronger than a
separating one.

5. *The Inner Planets:*   Because of the structure of the solar
system and the geocentric construction of the horoscope, Mercury
can never be more than 28° from the Sun, so only conjunction and
semi-sextiles are possible between the two. Venus can never be
more than 48° from the Sun, so that the semi-square is the widest
aspect possible. Mercury and Venus can never be more than 72°
from each other and therefore the sextile is the widest major aspect
possible between these two planets.

6. *Parallels:*   Declination is a planet's distance north or south of the Celestial Equator. Where two planets are at the same declination they are in parallel, a minor harmonious contact. Where they are at equal, but opposite declinations (e.g. 5° north and 5° south) they are contra-parallel, a minor inharmonious contact. Not all astrologers use parallels of declination, but it is worth noting that where there is also an aspect by zodiacal longtitude, then the influence of that aspect is strengthened by the parallel of declination.

7. *Aspect Patterns:*   Because astrology is a flowing, non-dogmatic science, often presenting paradox and mystery, many astrologers are tempted to latch onto neat formulae and clever systems. Whilst these can make valuable but subsidiary contributions to interpretation, the danger is that they act like fog lit up by a car's headlights, dazzling the driver and obscuring the road ahead. Chart shaping—'bowls, buckets, seesaws', etc.—is one such system which must be used with a sane sense of proportion. Aspect patterns are another. Such combinations as Grand Trines, T Squares, Grand Crosses and others are unquestionably important and need to be considered in interpretation, but many are the astrologers who have held out a chart (showing the aspect lines) with wide-eyed enthusiasm saying 'Look! A T Square, a finger of fate *and* a mystic rectangle!' The obscurer aspect patterns may well help certain astrologers to deepen their understanding of the chart, but often they act as diversions from the important, basic understanding of the chart—planets in signs, planets in houses and the aspects. Interpretation is often a hard slog through the unexplored and rocky terrain of the chart, unglamorous and unsensational, but it is normally there where the first real light of understanding begins to shine.

 The three major aspect patterns have been mentioned above. (In these cases the aspect lines should be drawn if the patterns are to be seen clearly). The Grand Trine involves three planets each in trine to the other and it brings a benignly harmonious flow of energy. But this pattern is not the ultimate gift from a benevolent deity, as some people suppose—it has an almost too pleasantly relaxed quality about it and work is needed if its potential is to be made use of in practice. Another normally anonymous pattern, which one might call a 'less grand trine' (Fig. 19), is formed by two sextiles and a trine—a small, flat isosceles triangle—and this can be considered a more benevolent pattern than a Grand Trine. A less

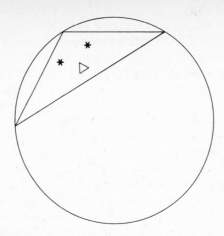

Figure 19.

easy, but more constructive combination is a triangulation of sextile, trine and opposition—the two easier aspects make a valuable contribution to the positive working out of the opposition (Fig. 20).

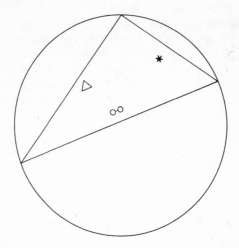

Figure 20.

The T Square is a stressful pattern of three planets forming an opposition and two squares. It is a challenging combination, but not necessarily the fearful influence that many people imagine.

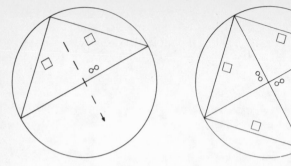

Figure 21.   *Figure 22.*

Sometimes a clue to the unlocking of the potential of the three T square planets can be found by concentrating on the 'empty' sign and house and its ruler opposite the planet receiving the two squares. (Fig. 21). In the case of the Grand Cross (sometimes referred to as Cosmic Cross) the empty quarter of the T Square is filled, so that a pair of oppositions and four squares link four planets in a strong cruciform shape (Fig. 22). This is an especially testing pattern and in some ways brings an extra Saturnian quality into the chart. The individual will have difficult lessons to learn and obstacles to overcome, but the evolutionary rewards are great if these lessons are confronted and absorbed. T Squares and Grand Crosses are usually in signs of the same quality and descriptions such as 'fixed cross' or 'cardinal T Square' are often given.

Nevertheless, the first step to interpreting any special aspect pattern is to consider each individual part which makes it up. Only then should the additional effect of the pattern itself be brought into the interpretation.

Finding the Aspects

Initially, many students are overwhelmed by the prospect of counting degree distances between planets, adding or subtracting orbs, in order to find each aspect. Skill comes quickly with experience, but there are certain short cuts and hints which are helpful:

1. Get into the habit of seeing the relationship between the signs in which the planets are placed—polarity, quality and element.
2. To find an aspect between two planets, use one of them in its degree and sign, as 'base'. Then look and see if the other planet is on the same degree of *its* sign, or within orbs either side.

3. Conjunctions should be obvious and oppositions usually involve the opposite sign.

4. Squares can be found by looking for a planet in or near the same degree of a sign of the same quality, three signs away. Trines involve the same element, four signs away. Sextiles involve the same polarity, two signs away.

5. Planets in quincunx and semi-sextiles, with smaller orbs, will be nearer the same degree number of their own sign, either five or one sign away respectively.

6. Watch out for dissociate aspects where the degree numbers may be apparently 'different' (29° and 1° for example) and the element and quality rule is confused.

7. To find semi-squares and sesqui-quadrates, add or subtract 15° from the 'base' planet's degree and look around the new degree in the appropriate sign for an aspecting planet.

8. A quintile is a sextile plus 12° and a septile is a sextile minus $10° + 1\frac{3}{7}°$.

Table of Aspects

All aspects represent a fusion of energy of the two planets involved. This can either be used beneficially or allowed to influence non-constructively.

Aspect	Symbol	Degree Distance	Orb	
Conjunction		0°	±8°	
Opposition		180°	±8°	
Square		90°	±8°	More challenging Aspects
Semi-Square		45°	±2°	
Sesqui-Quadrate		135°	±2°	
Quincunx		150°	±2°	
Trine		120°	±8°	
Sextile		60°	±5°	
Semi-Sextile		30°	±2°	Easier Aspects
Quintile		72°	±2°	
Septile		$51\frac{3}{7}°$	±2°	

Aspect Meanings

The following short interpretations for each aspect are summaries acting as pointers towards deeper synthesized delineations. At first the student astrologer will need to refer constantly to books throughout every chart analysis, but the mature astrologer will always use the basic principles to form his own interpretation, allowing them to flow out from within rather than relying on pigeon-holed paragraphs from text-books. This applies not only to aspects but to all interpretations. A useful, additional synthesizing approach to understanding the aspects is to convert the connection between the two planets to equivalent planet-in-sign alternatives—as if the one planet were in the sign ruled by the other or vice versa. Thus, an aspect between Mercury and Jupiter has a similar quality to Mercury in Sagittarius, Mercury in Pisces, Jupiter in Gemini and Jupiter in Virgo.

Aspect interpretation should always also take into account the sign and house placings and the houses ruled by the planets involved. The other aspects in the chart, and particularly other aspects to those planets, will also modify the pure expression of any one combination. The skill of synthesis is to see the chart as a complete tapestry rather than a mass of different multi-coloured threads.

The comments on each contact suggest both the more positive and the less constructive expressions. But always remember that any aspect between two planets has the potential for beneficial expression. The inharmonious aspects represent more of an uphill struggle and need more character and life work to be applied by the individual.

Sun-Moon: This aspect has to do with personal integration and balanced self-expression. The conjunction gives a single-minded confidence, a certain self-satisfaction and an equilibrium of individuality. Easier aspects bring a basic inner harmony, but which sometimes lacks drive. The more stressful aspects produce a feeling that life presents obstacles—a frustration which can cause restlessness.

Sun-Mercury: Of the two aspects possible, the semi-sextile, although minor, is often more favourable in giving mental balance and harmony since different signs are usually involved. The conjunction produces a strong intellect and forceful presentation of ideas, but the mind is often over-subjective and sometimes blinkered.

Sun-Venus: Charm, personal magnetism and a good aesthetic sense are given by this combination. Pleasantly extrovert, the individual will present a friendly warmth when in contact with other people. Inharmonious expression (only the semi-square is possible) can result in extravagence and indulgence.

Sun-Mars: Will, power, drive and the vital force express through this combination. Self-confidence and the knowledge that any tasks can be successfully tackled stem from a powerhouse of energy, but forcefulness and self-assertion can sometimes border on aggression. The less easy aspects in no way detract from the vitality and power, but produce difficulty in that the energy is almost too hot to handle. Results are expected instantly, the temper is short and an often selfish impatience governs the life. The sexual urge is strong in all cases, but prone to lack of control if the aspect is inharmonious.

Sun-Jupiter: Generosity, benevolence and good fortune are indicated. All life will be conducted with enthusiasm and on a grand scale—an infectious optimism colours everything contacted. The individual is always ready for any opportunity, looking towards the far horizons which represent the multiple possibilities of life—philosophies, travel and expansion. The harmonious aspects can often literally bring good luck, while the inharmonious contacts allow ostentatious extravagance, over-extending resources, self-indulgence and wastefulness. These usually result from an over-inflated attitude to life. Speculation is a great temptation, but poor judgement can cause it to end disastrously.

Sun-Saturn: Responsibility, seriousness and self-discipline are central to life, often resulting in delays to achievement. The individual may have matured early, developing a stoical reserve and a realisation of the need for hard work. The more harmonious aspects give sound common sense and a realistic approach to the material world. The individual is patient and methodical, deriving quiet pleasure from fulfilling his duty. The difficult aspects present tests and lessons to be learned, which may have the appearance of difficulties and obstacles to be overcome. Saturn's restricting influence often comes about as a result of under-confidence or a sense of under-achievement, both of which can be destructive unless confronted, understood and gradually transformed.

Sun-Uranus: Unconventional and unpredictable, almost to the point of eccentricity, the individual leads a life full of surprises, but he is original and inventive and has a friendly, humanitarian attitude. However, the restrictions of tradition and convention are not easily tolerated, for freedom, dynamism and progress are essential to him. Inharmonious aspects allow a disruptive, highly-strung quality to manifest. The individual can be erratic and irresponsible, often obtusely stubborn and irritable. Sudden changes will be a feature of life—the breaking of old structures in order to make room for the new.

Sun-Neptune: The individual is brought into contact with intangible forces, with other levels of perception and with inspiration and spirituality. Sensitivity is heightened, bringing with it impressionability, an easy-to-be-with quality, artistic appreciation and inspiration. A dreamy nature is usual and there will be interest in mysticism and illusion; psychic experiences may be encountered. The inharmonious aspects are difficult to handle because of the nebulous nature of the contact. Deception, escapism and over-idealism can seduce the individual into a misplaced sense of security and further confusion and dilution of reality results. Feelings of inferiority may produce an exaggerated need to please others and the individual often behaves like a chameleon.

Sun-Pluto: Powerful inner intensity gives the necessity for constant self-renewal. Life becomes a series of continuous rebirths and although the individual is largely introspective, the power-seeking side of Pluto can be domineering towards others. Extremism and a deep investigatory quality characterizes Sun-Pluto contacts. The difficult aspects intensify the power of Pluto, but also bring out a ruthless willful quality which can be highly destructive. Psychological earthquakes feature in the life, deep turbulence causing break-up on the surface—which can lead either to breakdown or breakthrough in self-development. But in either event rebirth still occurs.

Moon-Mercury: There is a strong need to respond to others in communication, often to the extent of being too adjustable and over-adaptable. Ideas will be communicated with sensitivity and awareness, but there is a restlessness and a feeling of inconsistency. The easier aspects will give a pleasant versatility, while the more difficult aspects allow moods and feelings to overcome the rational mind and manipulate facts in a whimsical fashion.

Moon-Venus: Grace, beauty and popularity are offered by this contact, like the charm of the elegantly successful hostess. Artistically sensitive, the individual is also likely to enjoy emotional relationships and feel warmly fulfilled in attachment. But there can be too pleasant, too sweet a response and where the aspects are inharmonious this can lead to difficulty in relationships. Exaggerated pleasure-seeking may not only bring extravagence and a love of luxury, but can also result in submissiveness and an eagerness to please at the expense of self-respect.

Moon-Mars: The emotions are strongly expressed with confidence, but often with sensitivity. This softening of personal drive can be very appealing, but where the aspects are inharmonious a quarrelsome, emotionally agitating influence is present. The individual can be selfish and bitchy, showing remarkable lack of sympathy to others.

Moon-Jupiter: Feelings and emotional response express warmly, generously and happily. The individual will be fun-loving and expansive, enjoying travel and the pleasures of life. Giving is a pleasure and optimism is seldom misplaced. The inharmonious aspects only tend to over-emphasize these qualities, resulting in exaggeration of feelings and a happy-go-lucky carelessness.

Moon-Saturn: Emotional expression and spontanaiety of feelings are restricted by any contact between these two planets. The harmonious aspects can bring emotional stability and common-sense, but there is always likely to be restraint and perhaps shyness. The more difficult aspects can result in cutting off the feelings, mistakenly seen as self-sufficiency, and the individual becomes stern, cold, brooding and even melancholic and depressed.

Moon-Uranus: There is a highly-charged emotional quality about the individual and, coupled with an originality of response, this often makes for a fascinating personality; also the harmonious aspects emphasise a refreshing openness and honesty. All this can be exciting and stimulating to other people, but under more stressful aspects impatience, impulsiveness and unpredictable emotional behaviour can occur. Inner emotional tension often results in a highly-strung, nervy disposition.

Moon-Neptune: This is an extremely sensitive combination, giving finely-tuned receptivity to the higher levels of inspiration. The individual is likely to be creative and artistic. Openess, almost to the point of vulnerability, gives a sympathetic nature and often results in mystical or psychic experiences. The less easy aspects are particularly deceptive and make it difficult for the individual to separate illusion from reality. His drifting moods cloud his sensitive feelings so that he is not only a poor judge of others, but also of his own reactions. Escapist tendencies need to be treated with care and there can be difficulties with women—or more broadly with the 'feminine principle'.

Moon-Pluto: The emotional life has great depths and feelings are expressed secretively, but with intensity. The easier aspects allow a penetrating understanding of human emotions and behaviour, which can be applied to others or to oneself as an aid to growth in consciousness. The inharmonious aspects can allow lower emotional reactions, like vindictiveness, hate and envy to dominate behaviour and there is often a desire to control others. Emotional explosions are common. But all contacts give the opportunity for transformation, changing the less controllable emotions into higher expressions of love and concern for one's fellow being.

Mercury—Venus: (These two planets cannot form any major aspect beyond the sextile; 72° is maximum distance apart.) The individual is a pleasant conversationalist and is likely to be charming and diplomatic. Interest in the arts and probably music is suggested and there is an appreciative sense of humour. Mental profundity is unlikely.

Mercury-Mars: The mind is active and very sharp. The individual will want to use this ability frequently and sometimes his mental agility has the appearance of instability. Arguments are enjoyed and sarcastic, cutting comments may often be used. There is a mental directness, both in thought and word, which is healthy and stimulating, but it can easily be experienced as tactlessness by a more sensitive recipient.

Mercury-Jupiter: Potentially the mind can encompass wide areas and present information and knowledge perceptively and enthusiastically to the world. But broadmindedness can easily develop into exaggeration and poor judgement. If the indiscriminate nature of the contact is allowed to operate too freely, facts can be used like a smoke-screen rather than as communication of information and misunderstandings may occur.

Mercury-Saturn: Potentially this contact can bring mental stability, organizational skill and a practical, consolidating intellectual approach. It can help concentration and study. The undesirable expression of the contact exaggerates these qualities and often indicates difficulty with early education. It usually also suggests a slow mind and an over-cautious, inhibited mental attitude which can bring pessimism, worry and a fear of intellectual commitment.

Mercury-Uranus: The mind is inventive and intuitive and may spark off a lightning flash of genius. But the division between brilliance and insanity is often thin and the individual can be highly-strung and impatient, putting forward ideas in an opinionated manner, but often without being understood. This makes him feel not that he is miscommunicating, but that he is ahead of his time; such compounded frustration may become rebelliousness.

Mercury-Neptune: A rich imagination is indicated, with the additional possibility of a visionary or psychic mind. Vague and intangible concepts can be 'understood' with a non-rational brilliance and the intellectual sensitivity of the contact suggests creative writing and poetry. But Neptune's influence can easily drift towards dreaminess and confusion; the imagination creates substitutions for reality and clouds logical thinking. Truth becomes adjustable and a subtly amoral deceptiveness is used automatically and with increasing lack of discrimination.

Mercury-Pluto: The mind works deeply, probing into the hidden recesses of knowledge, applying the skills of the detective, the code breaker and the psychoanalyst. Although this relentless, penetrating quality is thorough, it can also be obsessive and explosive, often manifesting in caustic comments or dictatorial behaviour. But the contact always gives the potential to transcend and transform through mental activity.

Venus-Mars: This combination links love and activity, joining the female symbol with male. Thus enjoyment of personal pleasures is indicated, sensual and sexual particularly. Harmonious expression of the contact brings romantic passion and an easy flow of energy in relationship, while the less constructive expression stimulates impulsive behaviour, an over-sexed quality and dissatisfaction or disappointment in relationships.

Venus-Jupiter: Contact between these two benevolent planets brings optimism, generosity and good fortune. The individual is pleasant to be with and enjoys having fun, but with the less easy aspects there is a quality of 'too much of a good thing'. It is easy to slide into extravagance, self-indulgence and waste, often with tasteless ostentation. Uncharacteristic discipline would be needed in such an instance to draw the best from the contact.

Venus-Saturn: At best this combintion stabilizes the affections, bringing loyal nature and long-standing relationships, often with an older partner or later in life. But is has a strong tendency to control the easy expression of love to the extent of withholding affection or blocking the ability to allow oneself to be loved. Under-confidence in relationship is suggested or, for a woman, underconfidence in her femininity and a vulnerability to criticism.

Venus-Uranus: Relationships are often entered unexpectedly and are prone to upheaval, change and sudden breaks. But the constructive side of the contact can be brought out in unconventional relationships and by feeding in the piquancy and excitement of the unexpected or bizarre. An element of friendship also needs to be allowed—the lovers should also be pals. Unusual artistic interests or talents are possible.

Venus-Neptune: Contact between Venus and its higher octave indicates artistic sensitivity and inspiration, often appearing as musical talent. Relationships may reach a higher almost spiritual level of expression where love is tender and refined. But Neptune can insidiously turn glamorous ideals into romantic illusion and emotional weakness, so that disappointment occurs or deceptions creep into the relationship.

Venus-Pluto: Relationship is the field of transformation and the person will involve himself with others using an intensity which is compulsive and may even be obsessive. Potentially he may seek to learn to love humanity through loving one person, but that partner may experience jealousy, violence, strange sexuality or a power struggle in what is likely to be an unavoidable, unforgettable coupling. Infatuations and dark fantasies are also suggested and artistic interests may be strange and profound.

Mars-Jupiter: Energy is expanded and enthusiasm is vitalized. Often the individual will have more drive than he knows what do with and will not be able to channel it harmoniously—over-indulgence, excitability and restlessness may result. But the cheerful vigour and liveliness is infectious and the contact brings tangible success from effort expended.

Mars-Saturn: A frustrating inner paradox, this contact may be able to stabilize energy expression, but it is more likely to cause difficulty in achieving ones aims. Hard work will be needed to realize ambitions and underconfidence or self-doubt will have to be overcome—usually by trying to hide from others any suggestion of weakness. A man may feel his masculinity is threatened and this can have such diverse results as harsh aggression, coldness, withdrawal or sexual difficulties. Accidents are possible.

Mars-Uranus: This is an unstable, explosive contact—it is as if the individual is handling a high voltage cable with inadequate insulation. It is certainly possible to channel and apply this power successfully in progressive and inventive directions, but the balance is delicate and it may easily topple into headstrong behaviour or violence. Tension and irritability are also suggested and sudden accidents are possible.

Mars-Neptune: It is possible to refine and uplift the more basic energies and to give practical manifestation to creative and idealistic ventures. But the contact is a confusing paradox and often it is difficult for the individual to apply himself in any constructive function. Inconsistency, bad judgement and a lack of objectives can lead to an attraction to negative aspects of the environment and to strange indulgencies. Weird sexuality, cruelty, self-destructiveness and drugs should all be treated with extreme caution.

Mars-Pluto: Energy is expressed powerfully and explosivly. The individual has an intense need to win whatever battle is being fought and this can result in either significant personal growth or self-destruction. The temper is strong or even violent and there is often a need to control or dominate. Sexuality is intense.

The Slower-Moving Planets

Any aspects between Jupiter, Saturn, Neptune, Uranus, and Pluto are within orbs for long periods of time and are not so directly relevant to personal interpretation unless there is additional contact with an angle or one of the faster-moving planets. For this reason only key word interpretations are given.

Jupiter-Saturn: Discipline and consolidation. Frustration and restlessness.

Jupiter-Uranus: Unrestrained enthusiasm and sudden good fortune. Dissatisfaction and lack of discipline.

Jupiter-Neptune: Sensitivity, inspiration and compassion. Overidealism, superstitution and gullibility.

Jupiter-Pluto: Truth-seeking and resourcefulness. Intolerance and self-gratification.

Saturn-Uranus: Transformation of traditions, efficient progressiveness. Anarchy and touchiness.

Saturn-Neptune: Practical idealism and spiritual responsibiity. Frustration and discontent.

Saturn-Pluto: Disciplined concentration. Control by force, intense austerity.

Uranus-Neptune: Paranormal and sudden illumination. Weird delusions and shattered consciousness.

Uranus-Pluto: Radical reform and inner awakening. Sudden annihilation.

Neptune-Pluto: Awakening of mass spiritual consciousness. Disintegration of foundations.

9.
MISCELLANEA

The Moon's Nodes

The Moon's Nodes are points in space where the orbit of the Earth intersects the orbit of the Moon. These two points are always opposite each other and are normally known as the North and South Nodes, but their other names possess ancient and magical sounds which perhaps reflect the fascination held by many astrologers for them—Dragon's Head or Caput Draconis; Dragon's Tail, Cauda Draconis or Katababazon. The Nodes regress through the zodiac faster than Saturn, but slower than Jupiter and take about 18½ years to complete a cycle. The symbols are ☊ and ☋ respectively.

Astrologers are by no means unanimous in their interpretations of the Nodes, but most recognize that these points do have a certain importance. In my experience the Nodes can contribute to additional understanding of the chart, subtle and sometimes elusive, but helpful nonetheless if the meaning can be intuitively grasped. Very often the meaning of the Nodes corresponds with another interpretative point in the chart and gives it a gentle emphasis and a deeper importance.

The North Node seems to be a point of potential fulfilment in the chart, by sign and house and through any planet which is in close aspect to it. But the promise of the North Node cannot be fully realized until the opposite point, the South Node, has been attended to. Thus the value of understanding the meanings of house and sign polarities is obvious, for this is the basis of Node interpretation. Any planet in close aspect to the North Node will of course also be in aspect to the South Node.

In some respects it helps to think of the South Node as an undemanding version of Saturn. It offers lessons to be learned, but does not threaten punishment if a choice is made to concentrate on other features in the chart. To use the Nodes actively is to squeeze something additional out of the birth chart. It is a pity to ignore them, for that would not be taking full advantage of the potential of the chart, but there is no penalty. Indeed, it is important to concentrate on the basics of the chart and on Saturn, both in interpreting for someone else and in working on oneself through one's own chart, before attempting to introduce the complex and subtle nodal harmonies.

The Parents

Our parents have enormous psychological influence on us. For the girl child the model of femininity is her mother and the first male with whom she establishes a relationship is her father. Similarly the boy child starts to find out about relating with women through his mother and his ideal of manhood starts off with the first male he encounters, his father. Some parents hold on to their children too tightly and do not prepare them for the world outside nursery and home. Others hold too loosely and do not give the children the early nurturing and stability they need in order to grow in confidence and towards a trusting maturity. Parenthood is the most responsible job any human being can carry out, but it is the easiest to take on and one for which no qualifications are required. A cynic might suggest that parents can never win—whatever they do they will inevitably have some sort of detrimental effect. The perfect parent cannot exist; the best that one can hope for is to be the 'good enough' parent.

Such is the importance of the parents that the birth chart must reflect their influence, whether one believes in the soul's choosing both the chart and the parents or in psychological correspondence symbolized by the planetary placings. Often the chart reflects the relationship with the parents with uncanny precision, but at other times the indications are less obvious. There are no hard and fast rules for this aspect of interpretation, but the definite indicators which do exist must be considered with an open awareness and with flexibility.

The main indicator is the polarity of 4th and 10th houses. Usually the 4th house represents the father and the 10th the mother, but in some cases it is reversed. Certainly the two houses together are the two parents together. Any planets in these houses may represent a parent and planets close to the cusps will be particularly strong—they will also be angular if a quadrant house system is being used.

The rulers of the two houses are relevant and their positions and aspects give further information. For example, where the ruler of the 10th house is found in the 4th house, it may mean that the mother also had to play the role of the father for some reason. Or more importantly, it may mean that the individual concerned experienced his mother in this way. The chart is more likely to show the subjective relationship with the parents, rather than the actual physical reality of the mother and father.

Saturn usually symbolizes the father and the Moon the mother. The Sun can also sometimes symbolize the father, particularly in a woman's chart. Thus, aspects to these planets and their chart placings must also be integrated into the interpretations taken from the 4th and 10th houses. An angular Saturn or Moon will nearly always point to a very strong influence from one of the parents—too close a relationship which holds the younger person back; a difficult or painful relationship; or even an influence caused by absence.

Sometimes a grandparent, aunt or other person took the place of a parent and this parental proxy influence may be what the chart is showing. The parent influence may have come from someone who was not a parent, from someone who was absent or inadequate or from a parent long since dead. Always the parent influence lives on and affects relationships with both men and women throughout life, impinging also on attitudes to masculinity and femininity. It is this broadness and complexity which the chart will be trying to show us if we can read it, but pigeon-holed analysis will not unlock the door, only a sensitively handled synthesis.

Mid-Points

Mid-points are used extensively by many modern astrologers and the system has the attraction not only of being one of the newer developments in astrology, but also one which has been researched with German efficiency and offers interpretations based on large numbers of case histories.

A mid-point between two planets can be taken as an additional sensitive point in the chart having a quality of the combination of the two planets even if they are not aspect. Thus, if an aspect is formed between a third planet and that mid-point, then it is as if the three planets are all in a type of aspect pattern. Only small orbs of 1½°-3° are used.

To use this system certain handbooks and a mid-point calculation dial are necessary—which sometimes represents a commitment to the system and a specialization which has a danger of squeezing out the many other approaches to chart interpretation. I recommend that students investigate this system and take it into their knowledge and experience, using it extensively or sparsely as seems appropriate to each of them.

The attitude to astrology which will aid synthesis is one which searches more deeply into such systems as mid-points. For example, two planets not in aspect in a chart may nevertheless be connected by a mid-point aspect pattern. Or an empty house may very well contain a number of mid-points which can possibly aid interpretation of that area of the chart. The mid-points system, precise and disciplined, reminds us that all the signs and all the houses have a degree of importance in any chart. It also reminds us that astrology is a subject which can embrace a wide range of different attitudes and different systems, all of which may have their uses and abuses, but all of which deserve consideration.

Arabian Parts

In ancient Arabian astrology, a number of hypothetical points in the horoscopes were calculated using various relationships between planets and angles. There are at least forty of these, but the one which is best known is the 'Part of Fortune' or Pars Fortuna—a point on the chart where benefit will accrue and happiness will be found.

It is calculated by adding the degree of the ascendant to the degree of the Moon and then subtracting the degree of the Sun. The other possible combinations which produce the other Parts are almost limitless and range from: 'Part of Commerce' (Ascendant plus Mercury minus Sun) and 'Part of Love' (Ascendant plus Venus minus Sun), to such perplexing combinations as 'Part of Understanding' (Ascendant plus Mars minus Mercury) and 'Part of Journeys by Water' (Ascendant plus 15° Cancer minus Saturn).

It can be an interesting exercise to examine the Parts in one's own chart, but there is such a plethora of them that it is impractical to use them in normal chart interpretation—one can create a nightmarish fantasy of a chart where each degree of the zodiac has at least one so-called important feature—part, planet, angle, node, mid-point etc.—making interpretation impossible.

But the 'Part of Fortune' (Fortuna) seems to have survived the deluge and its upraised head can sometimes be glimpsed above the sea of irrelevancies. The probable reason is that it acts as a pointer to the importance of the relationship between the Sun and the Moon in the diurnal location the the chart. There is not enough space here to elaborate on the meanings of the phases of the Moon, but the subject is certainly worth further study—Dane Rudhyar has written extensively in and around this area. Thus an appreciation of the principles *behind* any astrological subject such as the 'Part of Fortune' and active consideration of what these principles may lead to, will be much more help in developing skill in synthesis than finding a text book which gives interpretations of Fortuna, for example, by sign, house and aspect and learning the paragraphs off by heart.

This example may become clearer as we consider people born at a New Moon (Sun conjunct Moon) and at a Full Moon (Sun opposite Moon). The first chart will always have a Fortuna conjunct the Ascendant; the full-moon birth in the second chart places Fortuna conjunct the 7th house cusp. 'Benefit from personal matters' (Fortuna in 1st) correlates with the character integration and sign emphasis suggested in a chart with a Sun-Moon conjunction in the same sign. 'Benefit from relationships' (Fortuna in 7th) correlates with the tension of the Sun-Moon opposition and with the need to achieve a balanced expression between the two signs of polarity. It suggests that a close personal relationship or marriage may be the most readily available vehicle or material for working out the configurations of Sun opposite Moon and the polarity of the rising sign and the sign on the 7th house cusp.

10.
FINAL WORDS

It may help to summarize here the steps to be taken in interpreting a chart. The steps have been either mentioned or implied in preceding pages and this approach will help synthesis to develop out of pure analysis.

1. Look at the whole chart and gain an overall impression. Perhaps consider the shapings and groupings of the planets and, if aspect lines are drawn, observe aspect patterns. Look for any prominently placed planets.

2. Check the more general indicators—emphasis by polarity, element and quality. Observe Dignities, Exaltations, Detriments and Falls.

3. Start the chart interpretation at the Ascendant and perhaps consider any first house planets, especially if they are angular or placed in the same sign as the Ascendant.

4. Let the interpretation flow next either to the ruling planet or to the Sun or to any point on the chart which appears particularly strong. Continue in this manner.

5. Always look for qualitative links within the chart. For example, work and career stretch beyond merely 6th house and 10th house. Relationships are more than just Venus and 7th house. House rulers often provide the first stage of these qualitative links.

6. Look behind the conventional meanings and the text book definitions; search for the symbols within the chart. This will help synthesized interpretations and deeper understanding.

In the wider context, it is as well to remember that every serious astrologer is always a student. Some are further along one of the roads than others, but we are all continually learning. Astrology is a rich and living subject and any astrologer who believes he has stopped learning will soon become arrid and his skills become sterile and lifeless.

For the early student there are extensive opportunities to learn the subject more formally and perhaps to obtain a qualification. Many adult education institutes in U.K. offer astrology as a subject and there are various other courses available, the Faculty of Astrological Studies (worldwide by correspondence or classes in London), probably being the most comprehensive.

For other students there is a cornucopia of books to read, organizations to join and lectures and conferences to attend. Although practical experience and conversation or discussion with other astrologers is essential, no one can ever read too many books on the subject. I recommend reading literally any astrology book— but always read it with constructive criticism. Some books are definitely better than others and a few are worthless. Some good books will appeal to one astrologer and not another—the field is wide. I do not intend to give a reading list, but there are authors whose names are worth mentioning. Charles Carter, Margaret Hone, Alan Leo, Ronald Davison, Jeff Mayo, Llewellyn George and Marc Jones have all written useful or essential books. Newer or more unusual ground has been explored by Dane Rudhyar, John Addey, Stephen Arroyo, Liz Greene, Alan Oken, Joan Hodgson, Michael Meyer, Rheinhold Ebertin, Zipporah Dobyns, Barbara Watters and Marc Robertson. There are many more—if names are excluded it does not necessarily mean that they are not recommended.

Do not be seduced by 'clever systems'. By all means make friends with them, but be in control of the relationship. Use the system as an additional aid to interpretation, not as the only method relied on. As with books, the different methods, systems, house divisions, philosophies and styles of presentation will appeal to different people. So try what appeals to you and use what you feel comfortable with, but do not put on blinkers and stick in one narrow groove. Astrology is about linking and bridging and it embraces many different sorts of people. It has applications in every area of human experience and endeavour. It is ours to enjoy, but to take seriously; to rejoice in, but to respect the privilege of being an astrologer.

TABLE OF KEYWORDS

The Planets

Sun   Identity, conscious self-expression, power, authority.

Moon   Response, receptivity, instinct, emotions, moods.

Mercury   Communication—the written and spoken word, intellect, the mind.

Venus   Love, attraction, beauty, harmony.

Mars   Energy, drive, confrontation, assertiveness.

Jupiter   Expansion, opportunity, justice, religion, preservation.

Saturn   Lessons to be learned, responsibility, duty, restriction, limitation.

Uranus   Sudden or unexpected change, inventiveness, originality, revolution.

Neptune   Refinement, inspiration, mysticism, deception, confusion.

Pluto   Transformation, regeneration, death and rebirth, elimination, the phoenix.

The Signs

Aries: 'Primal energy expresses itself'.

Initiating	Simple directness	Aggressive/quarrelsome
Decisive	Self-interest	Impulsive
Leader and Pioneer	Assertive	Insensitive
Courageous		Impatient

Taurus: 'My nourishment grows naturally from the earth'.

Loyal and Trustworthy	Nature-Loving	Possessive
Productive	Earthy and Sensual	Slow and Stolid
Artistic	Conservative	Covetous
Calm and Composed		Obstinate

Gemini: 'The Mind communicates streams of information'.

Eloquent	Inquiring	Superficial
Versatile	Witty	Shifty and Amoral
Clear Thinker	Light and Cheerful	Lacks concentration
Alert		Excitable

Cancer: 'Loved ones are nurtured protectively'.

Sympathetic	Maternal	Touchy
Protective	Family and Security	Devious
Understanding	Containing	Emotional Blackmailer
Kind and Caring		Grasping

Leo: 'Solar energy shines out from my centre'.

Generous	Fearless	Arrogant
Self-Confident	Magnetic	Condescending
Warm	Easy-going	Vain
Creative		Imperious

Virgo: 'Service expresses through work'.

Dependable	Research	Critical
Hard worker	Prudent	Nervous and Apprehensive
Meticulous and Efficient	Differentiation	Prudish
Service		Calculating

Libra: 'Equilibrium is achieved through relationship'.

Gracious and Sociable	Partnership	Indecisive
Impartial and Diplomatic	Strategist	Hedonistic
Artistic	Charmingly persuasive	Bland
Affectionate		Argumentative

Scorpio: 'Extremes are purged in the fire and rise again'.

Penetrating	Secretive	Ruthless
Steadfast and tenacious	Passionate and intense	Suspicious and vindictive
Unflinching	Catharsis	Power-seeking
Deep regeneration		Destructive

Sagittarius: 'The arrow speeds on its quest to the far horizon'.

Enthusiastic and jovial	Independent	Exaggeration
Optimistic	Traveller	Blunt and boisterous
Sincere	Frank and open	Hypocritical
Teacher of Wisdom		Rash and irresponsible

Capricorn: 'With discipline the peak is reached and experienced'.

Sense of responsibility	Executive	Rigid and demanding
Organizer and builder	Ambitious	Authoritarian
Patient	Dignified	Avaricous
Spirit in matter		Gloomy and limited

Aquarius: 'New ideals are presented to humanity'.

Truth-seeker	Scientist and inventor	Cool and detached
Humanitarian	Brotherhood and equality	Eccentric
Friendly and gregarious	Progressive	Rebellious drop-out
Co-operative		Sceptical

Pisces: 'The self is sacrificed in the waters of redemption'.

Compassion and sensitivity	Idealistic	Confusion
Grasps intangibles	Self-sacrificing	Masochistic and submissive
Unselfish	Imaginative	Lacks individuality
Spiritual and mystical		Dreamy

INDEX

Air signs, 34, 36, 41, 45, 48
Angles, 65
Angular houses, 63
Angularity, 27, 117
Applying, 101
Aquarius, 48-9, 53, 56, 58, 70, 71;
    Ascendant in, 70; glyph, 48, 49;
    keynote, 49; keywords, 49;
    planets in, 70, 71, 74, 77, 80, 83,
    87
Archetypes, 9
Aries, 13, 40, 53, 54, 55, 56, 57,
    65, 68, 70; Ascendant in, 68;
    First Point of, 12; glyph, 40;
    keynote, 40; keywords, 40;
    planets in, 68, 70, 73, 76, 79, 82,
    85, 101
Ascendant, 13, 51, 59, 60, 65, 66,
    68, 118, 119
Aspect links, 21
Aspect patterns, 102
Aspects, 15, 94-114, 117
    dissociate, 101, 105; finding the,
    105; table of, 106; meanings of,
    106-114
Asteroids, 19

Cadent houses, 63, 64-5
Campanus house system, 60
Cancer, 13, 42-3, 51, 52, 55, 58,
    69, 71, 118; Ascendant in, 69;
    glyph, 42; keynote, 43;
    keywords, 43; planets in, 69, 71,
    73, 76, 79, 82, 85, 101

Capricorn, 47-8, 53, 56, 58, 66, 70,
    71; Ascendant in, 70; glyphs, 47;
    keynote, 48; keywords, 48;
    planets in, 70, 71, 74, 77, 80, 83,
    86
Cardinal signs, 37, 40, 42, 45, 57, 58
Celestial Equator, 102
Charles, H.R.H. Prince, 12
Chart shaping, 102
Collective energies, 27
Collective unconscious, 9
Computer analysis, 15, 16
Conjunction, 96, 101, 105, 119
Correspondences, 65
Cusps, 59, 64, 65, 70, 116, 119

Declination, 102
Descendant, 66
Detriment, 66, 67, 71, 74, 76, 77,
    79, 82, 85
Dignity, 66, 71, 73, 76, 79, 80, 83,
    86, 87
Duality, 33-4; see also Positive signs,
    Negative signs

Edison, Thomas, 28
Earth signs, 34, 35, 41, 44
Eighth house, 63, 64, 65; planets in,
    72, 75, 78, 81, 84, 88, 90, 91, 93
Elemental signs, 54
Elements, 34-6, 39, 98, 100, 101,
    105; see also Fire, Earth, Air and
    Water signs
Eleventh house, 63, 64; planets in,
    73, 75, 79, 81, 84, 89, 90, 92, 93

Equal House system, 60
Exaltation, 66-7, 71, 73, 77, 80, 82, 86

Fall, 67, 71, 74, 76, 79, 83, 85
Fate, 9
Fifth house, 61, 64; planets in, 72, 75, 78, 81, 84, 88, 90, 91, 92
Fire signs, 34, 35, 40, 43
First house, 61, 63, 119; planets in, 72, 74, 77, 80, 83, 87, 89, 91, 92
Fixed signs, 37, 41, 43, 45, 48
Fourth house, 61, 64, 116, 117; planets in, 72, 75, 78, 81, 84, 87-8, 90, 91, 92
Free will, 9

Gemini, 41-2, 52, 55, 57, 59, 69, 71; Ascendant in, 69; glyph, 41, 42; keynote, 42; keywords, 42; planets in, 69, 71, 73, 76, 79, 82, 85, 101, 106
Grand Cross, 102, 104-5
Grand Trine, 102

Herschel, Sir John, 28
Higher octave, 27, 28
Horoscope, analysis of, 7, 14, 16, 18, 68; function of, 11; structure of, 11-13
Houses, 14, 15, 59-67; see also under individual houses
House systems, 59

Imum Coeli (I.C.), 66
Individual signs, 64
Inner planets, aspects between, 101

Jung, C. G., 8
Jupiter, 19, 24-5, 26, 52, 53, 57, 58, 100, 106; aspect interpretations, 107, 109, 111, 112, 113, 114; glyph, 25; in houses, 83-5; in signs, 82-3; keywords, 25

Keats, John, 19
Keywords, 15, 16, 20, 21, 23, 24, 25, 26, 28, 29, 31, 39, 40, 41, 42, 43, 44, 45, 46, 47, 48, 49, 50
Koch house system, 60

Leo, 43-4, 51, 52, 55, 58, 69, 70, 71; Ascendant in, 69; glyph, 43; keynote, 43; keywords, 44; planets in, 69, 71, 73, 76, 79, 82, 85
Libra, 13, 45, 52, 55, 57, 65, 69, 71; Ascendant in, 69; glyph, 45; keynote, 45; keywords, 45; planets in, 69, 71, 74, 76, 79, 82-3, 86
Life energies, 14
Lowell, Percival, 30

Mars, 19, 23-4, 30, 52, 53, 54, 57, 65, 95, 101, 118; aspect interpretations, 107, 109, 110, 112, 113-4; glyph, 24, 28; in houses, 80-2; in signs, 79-80, 101; keywords, 24
Mercury, 19, 22-3, 28, 30, 52, 58, 74, 101, 106, 118; aspect interpretations, 107, 109, 110-12; glyph, 22; in houses, 74-6; in houses, 74-6; in signs, 73-4; keywords, 23
Midheaven, 60, 65-6
Mid-points, 117-8
Moon, 11, 12, 13, 15, 18, 19, 20-1, 51, 52, 58, 66, 101, 117, 118, 119; aspect interpretations, 109-10; glyph, 21; in houses, 72-3; in signs, 70-2, 101; keywords, 21; Nodes of the, 115-6; phases of the, 119
Mutual Reception, 101
Mutable signs, 38, 41, 44, 49

Negative signs, 33, 34, 41, 42, 44, 45, 49
Neptune, 12, 19, 28-9, 30, 52, 54, 58; aspect interpretations, 108, 110, 111, 112, 113, 114; glyph, 29; in houses, 91-2; keywords, 29
Ninth house, 63, 65; planets in, 72, 75, 78, 81, 84, 88-9, 90, 91, 93
Nodes, 115-6
Number symbolism, 94, 100

Opposition, 97, 103, 105, 119
Outer planets, 27, 89-93
Orbs, 100-1, 105, 117

Parallels of declination, 102

Parents, influence of, 116
Parts (Arabian)
  Part of Commerce, 118; Part of
  Fortune (Pars Fortuna), 118, 119;
  Part of Journeys by Water, 118;
  Part of Love, 118; Part of
  Understanding, 118
Pisces, 49-50, 53, 54, 56, 58, 70,
  72; Ascendant in, 70; glyph, 49;
  keynote, 50; keywords, 50; planets
  in, 70, 72, 74, 77, 80, 83, 87,
  106
Placidus house system, 60
Planetary strengths, 66-7
Planets, 14, 15, 18-31, 32, 33,
  51-4, 64, 65, 66; aspect
  interpretations, 106-114; in
  houses, 72-3, 74-6, 77-9, 80-2,
  83-5, 87-93; in signs, 68-72,
  73-4, 76-7, 79-80, 82-3, 85-7
Pluto, 12, 19, 29-30, 52, 54, 57;
  aspect interpretations, 109, 110,
  111-12, 113, 114; glyphs, 30; in
  houses, 92-3; keyword, 31
Polarity, 34, 57-8, 98, 100, 105,
  119
Positive signs, 33, 34, 40, 41, 43,
  45, 48, 57
Prana, 36

Quadrant house systems, 60, 65, 116
Qualities, 37-8, 39, 98, 100, 105;
  see also Cardinal, Fixed and
  Mutable signs
Quincunx, 100, 105
Quintile, 100, 105

Reincarnation, 8-9
Rising sign, see also Ascendant
Rudhyar, Dane, 119

Sagittarius, 46-7, 53, 56, 57, 59, 70,
  71; Ascendant in, 70; glyph, 46;
  keynote, 47; keywords, 47; planets
  in, 70, 71, 74, 77, 80, 83, 86,
  101, 106

Saturn, 19, 25-6, 27, 52, 53, 58,
  95, 104, 115, 117, 118; aspect
  interpretations, 108, 110, 111,
  112, 113, 114; glyph, 26; in
  houses, 87-9; in signs, 85-7,
  101; keywords, 26
Scorpio, 30, 45-6, 53, 54, 55, 56,
  57, 66, 69, 71; Ascendant in, 69;
  glyph, 45, 46; keynote, 46;
  keywords, 46; planets in, 69, 71,
  74, 77, 80, 83, 86
Second house, 61, 64; planets in, 72,
  75, 78, 80, 83, 87, 89, 91, 92
Semi-sextile, 100, 101, 105
Semi-square, 99, 101, 105
Separating, 101
Septile, 100
Sesqui-quadrate, 99, 105
Seventh house, 61, 63, 119; planets
  in, 72, 75, 78, 81, 84, 88, 90,
  91, 93
Sextile, 98-9, 101, 103, 105
Signs, 14, 15, 32-50, 51-8, 64, 66
Sign sympathies, 21
Sixth house, 61; planets in, 72, 75,
  78, 81, 84, 88, 90, 91, 93
Solar system, 11, 12
Square, 98, 99, 105
Succedent houses, 63, 64
Sun, 11, 12, 13, 15, 18, 20, 21, 22,
  51, 52, 58, 59, 68, 100, 101,
  117, 118, 119; aspect
  interpretations, 107-9; glyph, 20;
  keywords, 20
Sun signs, 65
Synastry, 21
Synchronicity, 8
Synthesis, 7, 8, 14, 16, 18, 67, 68,
  106, 118

Taurus, 41, 52, 54, 55, 57, 68-9,
  71;
  Ascendant in, 68-9; glyph, 41;
  keynote, 41; keywords, 41; planets
  in, 68-9, 71, 73, 76, 79, 82, 85,
  101
Tenth house, 63, 64, 116, 117;
  planets in, 73, 75, 78, 81, 84,
  89, 90, 92, 93

Third house, 61, 65; planets in, 72, 75, 78, 81, 83-4, 87, 90, 91, 92

Topocentric house system, 60

Trine, 97-8, 99, 101, 103, 105

T squares, 102, 103-4, 105

Twelfth house, 63, 65; planets in, 73, 76, 79, 82, 84-5, 89, 90, 92, 93

Universal signs, 54

Uranus, 12, 19, 27-8, 30, 52, 53, 58; aspect interpretations, 108, 111, 112, 113, 114; glyph, 28; in houses, 89-90; keywords, 28

Venus, 19, 23, 52, 57, 66, 100, 101, 118; aspect interpretations, 107, 109, 110, 112-3; glyph, 23; in houses, 77-9; in signs, 76-7, 101; keywords, 23

Virgo, 44, 52, 55, 58, 69, 71; Ascendant in, 69; glyph, 44; keynote, 44; keywords, 44; planets in, 69, 71, 73, 76, 79, 82, 86, 106

Water signs, 34, 36, 42, 45, 49

Yin-yang, 21, 34

Zodiac, 12, 13, 27, 29, 32, 33, 37, 39, 54, 59, 96, 97, 98, 110, 118

Zodiacal longitude, 102

The Faculty of Astrological Studies

The Faculty of Astrological Studies was founded in 1948 for the purpose of improving astrological knowledge and raising standards through courses of tuition and by examinations. There are correspondence courses for both Certificate and Diploma levels, offering personal tuition of a high standard to students anywhere in the world, and evening classes are also held in London, England. Certificate and Diploma exams take place each year and are open to Faculty students and others alike. The Diploma of the Faculty (D.F.Astrol.S.) is internationally recognized and is one of the most respected astrological qualifications in the world.

For further details write to:

The Registrar,
Faculty of Astrological Studies,
84b Wakeman Road,
London NW10 5DH